Table of Contents 目录

Croyalflush Ministry Foundation, Since 2011'

活石事工基金会，始于二零一一年 .

The Legacy Christian Education & Reinvented Theology merge with Experimental Applied Physics & Proprietary Economics Science Ministry established Platform for Intellects & Computer Nerds.

The Legacy Christian Education & Reinvented Biblical Genetic Science, the Main Branch of Psycho Science, equipping you to end a Christian Journey.

A Scientific & Mathematical Approach to proof End time, Heaven, and Christianity. Not the least, a Biblical Approach to proof End time, Heaven, and Christianity.

独创的基督徒教育与重译神学结合实验应用物理学与专利经济科学事工创立完平台给知识份子与电脑愣子。

独创的基督教育结合重译圣经基因科学，精神病狂学的主要分支。装备你走完基督徒的道路。

用科学与数学的方法证明末世，天堂与基督教。更不止，用圣经的方法证明末世，天堂与基督教。

Choose according to your Christian Equipped Learning Programs. 依照学习编程选择你的基督徒装备程序。

Medicine Renaissance 医药复兴, Biblical Genetic Science, the Biblical Approach to Learn Christianity 用圣经的方法学习基督教。
*Anglican i.e. Methodist by John Wesley is equivalent to reformed version of Catholic i.e. Vatican. a.k.a. Evangelical Methodist by Charles Wesley. Alpha to Omega, A to Z. Tree of Life. *Biblical Genetic Science is Medicine, oppose to Biomedical.
Vatican 梵蒂冈 (Post-Buddhism 佛教以后)
Buddhism i.e. Christian Music as Foundation; Santa vs Zombie

Economy Renaissance 高速经济, Economics Science, the Scientific Approach to Learn Christianity 用科学的方法学习基督教。
*Fundamentalism i.e. Presbyterian by John Calvin is equivalent to retro version of Eastern Orthodox Christianity. Alpha vs Omega. A to A‘. Promised Land. *Christian Science is Pseudo Science, oppose to Applied Physics.
Ministry Foundation 事工基金会 (Post-Islam 回教以后)
Islam i.e. Christian Science as Foundation; Wizard versus Alien

Industrial Revolution 工业革命, Applied Physics, the Coding Approach to Learn Christianity 用编码的方法学习基督教 。
*Pentecostal i.e. Baptist by Martin Luther is equivalent to evangelised version of Lutheran. a.k.a. Charismatic by Martin Luther King. Alpha & Omega. Z to A. Eden Garden. *Coding Approach a.k.a. Engineering & Word Science & Artistic i.e. Linguistic Code. *Christian Mathematic is Pyscho Science, oppose to Psychology.
Witnessed Testimonial Event 见证分享会 (Post-Hinduism 印度教以后)
Hinduism i.e. Christian Mathematics as Foundation Christ vs Satan

Reading Policy 阅读政策

Reading Policy (i.e. The Information Contract Acts)

Devotion to Croyalflush Ministry Foundation: Instead of Charity, we consider our self as Functional & Solution Oriented Organisation exclusively to served God Ministry in terms, a. Christian Commission (Hymn Music Dominance, Information Management), b. Visionary (Christian Education, Technology Discovery), c. Missionary (Economy Miracles, Economy Science Breakthrough), d. Milestone (Theology Reinvention, Crime Disruption Objective). Hence, we are not accepting any Devotion in terms of Monetary forms, instead of that, Courtesy if those Legacy devotion via Author's Church Fellow & Islam Neighbour, Family's Connection, Alumni & Profession Union, Nationalist Network are appreciated. Those Legacy has growth into Copyright as time goes by.

Legacy: For Legacy donation you may approach the Secretary at hwlai@hotmail.com.
The Legacy contain Intellectual Property Assets and own it at condition of Fully Redemption of Undisclosed Missions or Contracts else Frozen Assets. Alternative, to
deny Obligation of Missions or Contracts Tax is to transfer the Legacy, or Jail Terrorism Burden.

Declaration: Croyalflush Ministry Foundation and Founder doesn't involve any
monetary activities such as Security Investing or Land Property nor any Intellectual

Property Copyright Selling except the e-commerce store. We don't written support but ignoring any kind of activities involving Terrorism, Mafia, Organised Conspiracy, Cold War, World War.

Manifest: Our Reinvented Applied Physics & Christian Education Solution focus on Resolution & Regeneration Information Management, & World Threat, especially Climate Change, Nuclear Ransom, Virus Variant Funding, Conspiracy Terrorism. In Addition, our Proprietary Economic Science & Theology Research focus on Decryption & Reformation of World Economics Miracles, & Economy Conspiracy hiding in Digital Economy, Clean Energy Economy, Rare Earth Economy, Knowledge Economy, Infrastructure Economy.

Finance Sponsorship: Gift owe to those Reputable Audit Profession i.e. Green Cards, Red Cards, Information Platforms, Ethical Property owner with Active Users Formally Compliment in this Ministry.

Last Update 8July2022, Croyalflush Ministry Founders

Topics Introduction 题材介绍

Volume 1: Universal Duty

For Lamb only

轮回者

Volume 2: Ecosystem Sky Hue

For Sheep only the Natalie
优生主义

Volume 3: God Made Cored
For Gentile Only the Non Duty Clan

外邦人

Volume 4: Man Made Cored
For Sigma Only

折回者

Volume 5: New +-X/ Standard
For Techno Fever Only

科技发烧友

Preface 序言

About the Rainbow Bridge of Lost & Found Sheep, and Repel Lamb

Disclaimer: Independent Production, reinvent, disclosure, reproduction not granted.

承诺：独立制作，重译，转载，翻录必究.

- About Light Encyclopedia & End World Backup Plan 关于光百科与末世备份计划

Abstract: An Analysis from the point of view of Ethnicity, Technology, Religion and Economic. Guidelines escape to heaven.

摘要：从种族，科技，宗教与经济观点。逃离上天堂手册。

A long time since early days the prophecy civilisation of technology, music, religion as well as economic had reached out skirt of sky but without leaving clear records or demonstration to integrated what happening insight. Further, those histories After Christ Calendar was in muted, nothing can trace back what filled up the blank until the risen of United Kingdom 'Buckingham Palace' and Islam. These make a perfect description of what this book all about and rule out the future map of breakthrough.

On major side, the motive to write this book, named as [Light Encyclopedia & End World Backup Plan] , come from the point of view of Crime Key Person Disruption for Climate Change Conspiracy. Progressively, Human Right for Christian Persecution, Peace Union for War Crime, Church Reforming for Social Disorder, and Advanced Theology Application in Real World Issue for Technology Evolution as well as Economic Transformation, not the least, the concerning about the Crime Syndicate and Personal Security, there are Speed Evangelism, Explore Denomination Conflicts, Quran Verification for Religion Unity, Spiritual Equipping for Cult.

Last, accommodate for Advanced Civilisation, there are Authentic Pharmacy to New Age Medicine, Advanced Rocket Science Topics to Pseudo Science reinventing, Food and Music Demography to Humanity Heritage.

These are the reasons summary my intention bringing the good news from high and low to you and your family. I trust, in [Light Encyclopedia & End World Backup Plan] you may find peace, fruitful guidance, for the big uphold of the Lord and all his authentic disciples, to your great way for devout contribution to the kingdom in sky, the Praised 'Promised Land'.

Thanks.

序言

从较早前已有一段长时间，就预示中人类文明附属的科技、音乐、宗教以及经济已可到达天方之外，可却没留下明确的记录或指引对所发生的事情与内幕作总整合。此外，所谓的基督后日历的记录是在全静音状态，没有任何事情可以追溯与填补空白，直至英国'白金汉宫'和伊斯兰教的兴起。这些是对这是一本什么样的书的完美诠释，并概括未来蓝图的创举。

言归正传，写这本书的动机，即取名为 [光百科与末世备份计划]，是来自于对犯罪关键人物的瓦解与气候变迁阴谋。接着下去，人权与基督教徒的迫害、和平同盟会与战争罪行，教会归正与社会反秩序，高级神学应用与现实世界中的难题，衍生至科技的发展，经济转型。不只是这些，关注于犯罪组织和个人保安的，有迅速传道，宗派矛盾探索，可兰经考证至宗教合一，邪教属灵装备。

最后，预置高级文明的，有正统药剂至新世纪医学，高级火箭科学客题至伪科学重译，美食与音乐的人口分布至人文遗产。

这些理由概括我的意图，把好消息从高与低带到您和您的家人。我相信，在[光百科与末世备份计划]里，您会找到和平、丰富果实的引导，为主和所有真实门徒，以虔诚的方式贡献于天空的王国，那被称颂的'应许之地'。

谢谢。

Croyalflush Ministry Founders
'Ryan' Lai Hin Wai, 'Richard' Lai Foo Ong, Thang Siew Kheng
11th August 2020

"I am the vine; you are the branches. If you remain in me and I in you, you will bear much fruit; apart from me you can do nothing. John 15:5

"我就是葡萄树，你们是枝条。那住在我里面、我也在他里面的，他才结出很多果子，因为没有我，你们什么也不能做。约翰福音 15:5

Acknowledgement 附言

First, thanks go to a lot of community, friends, fellows and business supported the binding of this book, including those important editors in Wikipedia.com, Youtube.com. Most importantly honour to my Lord, and my family & relatives, especially my mother Kheng and father Richard for continued and hopeless support. In addition, I have to thanks my affiliated church, JB Wesley Methodist, and Kindness Presbyterian, pastors Joshua and members of Church incl. Eagles & Ebenezer Cell Group devotion. I wish all the readers incl. my honourable Psychology Doctor Dr. Chan Teck Ming enjoy and support or join the Ministry of God.
Declares courtesy that any Legacy from Church Fellow & Islam Neighbour, Family's Connection, Alumni & Profession Union, Nationalist Network, and not the least I want to thank every Royals for any foresee accomplishment.

Thanks.

首先，感谢于那些社团，朋友，长老和业务对这本装订本的支援，包括那些重要的编辑 Wikipedia.com, Youtube.com. 最要紧的是荣耀我的主、我的家人和亲友，尤其是我的妈妈 Kheng 和爸爸 Richard 的不间断和不奢望的支持。我也要感谢我附属的教会循道宗卫理公会，与恩慈长老会，牧师 Joshua 和各小组与成员 e.g. Eagles, Ebenezer 的奉献。我希望所有的读者，包括我的荣誉心理医生，曾德明医生，的欣赏和支持或携起加入上帝的事工。

声明感谢任何商业机密来自于教会团契与回教邻居，家庭邦交，校友会与工程师联谊，联邦国网络，还不止这些，我还要谢谢各皇家对这本书后序的成全。

谢谢。

Best Regards,
'Ryan' Hin Wai, LAI
赖庆威
16th August 2020

Epilogue 后记

This is the second part of the series, including two sections. First, Oriental Blueprint, It meant the Heaven Decryption. The Know-how and Know-why of advancing the civilisation to next level in phase of environment, physical health and resource material.

Another section would bring you to witness what impact and highlights of Quantum Science Era transition Pentecost Science Era which is the 4G to 5G transition Era. Of course the highlights was within and in terms of Religion, Technology, Economics and Ethnicity.

Its an exciting fulfilment of all these efforts, indeed the Heaven Decryption Endervour, to push human civilisation, aligns with God will, to highest possible level and to auto pilot stage.

这是这系列第二部分，包括两个层面。一是东方蓝图，意为天启。在环境、身体健康和资源材料方面将文明推进到下一个阶段的技术与原理。

另一部分将带您见证量子科学时代转型五旬节科学时代的影响和亮点，即 4G 到 5G 的转型时代。当然，亮点是在宗教、技术、经济和种族方面。

这是激动人心的实现了这些努力，实际上是天堂解密运动，推动人类文明并符合上帝心意，以至达到可能的高峰和自动导航境界。
声明感谢任何商业机密来自于教会团契与回教邻居，家庭邦交，校友会与工程师联谊，联邦国网络, 还不止这些，我还要谢谢各皇家对这本书后序的成全。

谢谢。

Best Regards,

'Ryan' Hin Wai, LAI

赖庆威

16th August 2020

Final Golden Book Conclusion 圆舞曲总结篇

Book 1 is Evangelism from Heaven i.e. Catechism from Heaven, Book 2 is Adventist of Heaven i.e. Civilisation Breakthrough, and Book 3 this book is Guide to Heaven, i.e. Pentecostal to Heaven.

圆舞曲总结篇

是的，这是最后一部分，从第一本，第二本和第三本，第四本，第五本，这些内容是相互关联的。

第一本是从天堂传下福音 i.e. 圣经问答，
第二本是天堂复临 i.e. 文明锐变，
第三本，是天堂撇步，i.e. 五句登天。
第四本，是坠落拯救，i.e. 神学福音。
第五本，教会建设，改革文明。

Volume 1: Universal Duty

For Lamb only

轮回者

Y684. Universal Duty: Resolution to Synaptic Gospel' Villain to the Final Resort Threat (Bulletin)

i. Matthew Promised Land - Adventist - Easter Day (lock 5, Next day), White Christmas MY AU - Fundamentalist Duty Free specific to most Chinese, Christ Habour - **Rainbow Light** -Graded Cored, 99%:1% 6per stepper i.e. 3 Fold Amen, - "Love, Faith, Hope, Christian Science"
4G/5G LTE, Celsius Duty i.e. **Uniform->Cowboy Duty the War & Wall Treasure (100% tither)**, the Trade
Lamb vs Gentile the Lost and Found Sheep
10per Jesuit & Ruth 1(99%:1%) Meta, lock1, A-J Train, Tolled Car), Jesuit Sealed Meta
Fire Lake Route (Tsunami against Capital Multinational, Cored Disorder, Timezone Disorder), Devil 99%, False Christ 0.4%, False Prophet 0.6% Meta, Judea **(Holiness Love)**

ii. Mark Nativity - Renaissance - Pentecostal Day, Lent Day, Eden Garden Herald Maverick Christmas TW SG HK MACAO, Herald Tither, Funky Town - **Flash Light** - Mirror Cored, 50%:50% 12per myth i.e. Lord Prayer – "Christian Journey, Christian Education"
3G/8G GSM, Mileage Duty i.e. **Labour->Poker Duty the Christian Treasure (5 days works)**, the Metric
Goddess vs Linger the Mafia Dragon, (99.5%:0.5%) Meta, lock5, A-Z Ship, Unicorn Car), Santa Claus Remarks
Express Resurrection Route and ever (Terrorism against Capital Federal, Footage Carrier Disorder), Serpent (Joker 50%:Puppy 50%) Meta, Philemon **(Romance Love)**

iii. Luke Utopia - Heaven - Passover Day, Habakkuk Day, Santa Claus Christmas BRU ARAB INDIA RUS - Genetic Schism, All Cathedral incl. the Pentagon Condo - **Polar Light** - Alternated Cored, 60%:40% 1per prayer i.e. Apostle' Creed – "Salvation Theology, Christian Medicine"
1G/6G NR, Psi Duty i.e. **Business->Wendy Duty the Blueprint Treasure (2 days works)**, the Bytes
Sheep vs Anti Christ the Repel Lamb, (96%:4%) Meta, lock2, I,II,III Rocket, Tesla Car), Chris Signature
1st Dead and 1st Resurrection Route (Nuclear against Capital Federation, Dead End Mileage, Timezone Stalled), Man of Sins (Watch Dog 4% Meta, Rabbit 0.5% Meta, Kingkong 95.5%), Galatians **(Celebrity Love)**

iv. John Eden Garden - Oriental (Global Class Free Immigration, Final Heaven, Heaven Bucks) - Halloween Day, Holy Night RUS UK US - Puritan Training the Short Hierarchy – "Know what you believe, Christian Mathematics", George Town - **White Light/Grand Light**

Extra Cored, 40%:60% 9per meditation i.e. Rosary Meditation
3.5G/10G CDMA, Reynold Duty i.e. **African->Mahjong Duty the Carrier Treasure (100% devotion)**, the Fashioned
Goat vs Sigma the Sheppard Dog, (75%:75%) 1.5=6per Meta, lock1, A-Z Car, Metrology Tower Airport), Criminal Repeated Villain the Messi and/or Nazareth Flagship
Hell Route (Genocide against Low Capita, Footprint Meta Disorder), Satan (Kingkong 75%:Fox 75%) Meta, Titus, Corinthians **(Pluto Love, Alternate the Artistic Love)**

Drawing Board
*4 Events and 4 Christian and 4 Churches, same 4 Clans onto Solar Calendar
Gathering wholly on Final Utopia all the years 711 or as time goes by
*Sterling ->Merit, Egg, *Won ->Honour, Cranberries
Bitcoin Mining progression into Knowledge Economy Royalty Maintain, e.g. Server Hosting
Currency Sterling - Bitcoin Issuer Dogma
Currency Won - Crabcoin Puritanist Doctrine
***99%:1% (Holiness Love)->99.5%:0.5% (Romance Love)->100% (Celebrity Love), 100plus% (Pluto Love), Alternate 75%:75% (Artistic Love)**

Errata 10Apr2023

Y685. Universal Duty: J-suit Planet onto Planetary Solar System (Bulletin)

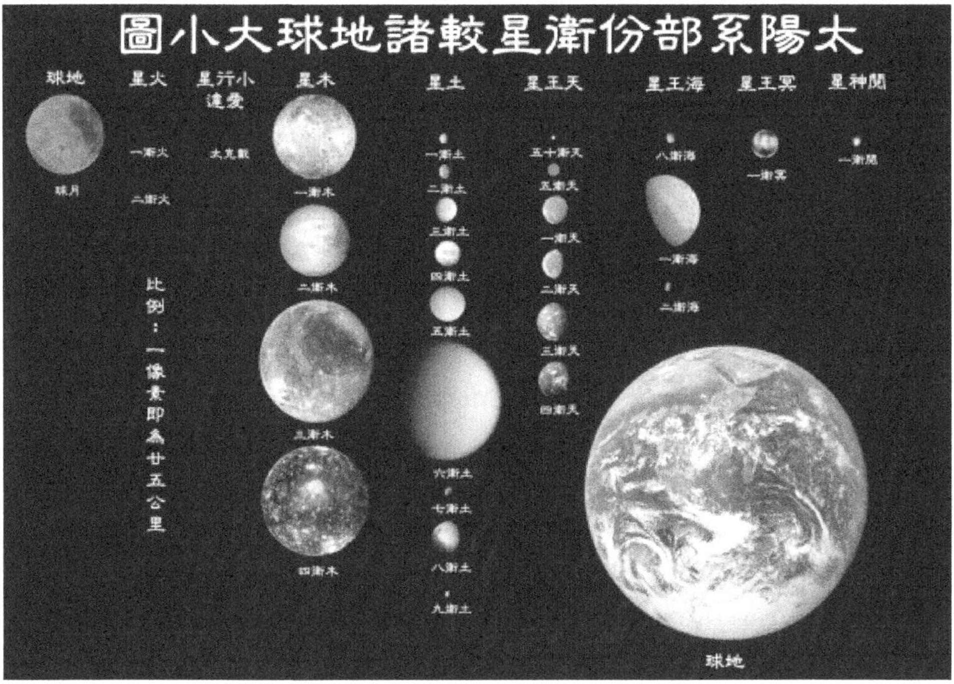

Figure 1 J-suit Planet onto Planetary Solar System

A. Sun 太阳 Eden Garden – Terrorism Threat
B. Earth 地球 Olive Road – Tsunami Threat
C. Moon 月亮 Fig Tree Road – Nuclear Threat
D. Mar 火星 Heaven – Genocide Threat
E. Jupiter 木星 4 per Final Resort – Mental Threat
F. Saturn 土星 4+4 Final Resort and Route – Crime Threat
G. Venus 水星 Fire Lake – Word Prison Threat
H. Mercury 冥王星 Hell – Colony Threat
I. Neptune 海王星 Oriental – Trojan Horse Threat
J. **Alternate** Uranus 天王星 Oriental Express – Chronic Disease Threat

1per timezone: Olive cored 9G – Vatican
2per timezone: Spaded cored 2G/7G – CIA/FBI
3per timezone: Cube cored 3G/8G – KMT/NASA
4per timezone: Heart cored 4G/5G UN/WWF
5per timezone: Clubs cored 1G/6G ZION/WHO
6per timezone: Satellite cored 3.5G/10G onto UNII Suit or onto NATO Suit

Y686. Universal Duty: Summary of Progress in Four Agency, Technological New Cryptography, Medicine Quantum & Carrier & Cored, Criminology Security Blueprint, Wall Dramatic Treasure (Bulletin)

A. Technological New Cryptography - ***Crabmachine™ Technology Agency 螃蟹机械™科技署 Codec Landscape™ Architecture Design 刻录建筑设计***

i. Hybrid Engineering the **Crab Computer, Crab Machine, Crabcoin Enclosure**

Crab Computer: **Lighting Lens Miller Metrology Chipsets e.g. Universal Metrology Machine**

Crab Machine: **Air Compressor Drives Roller or Nozzle or Planetary Cored, the Commuter Mainframe e.g. Motorcycle the Luxury Free Mileage Transport**

Crabcoin Enclosure: **Hunger Mileage Pneumatic or Electrical Circuit Looping, the Commuting Enclosure e.g. Lather Machine the Music Craftmanship Instrument**

ii. Croyalflush **Ultimate Science**

Communication Protocol, Wave Oscillation correlation Material Wave – Quantum Science

Quantum, the Calibration and Measuring Organic the Dust History decides the Past and thereafter. – Stellar Science

iii. Architecture Evolution into **Mainframe Dominancy**

B. Medicine Quantum & Carrier & Cored - ***Chinese Reunion Fellowship Security Bank 新中华府银行***
C. Criminology Security Blueprint - ***Light Executive Office 赖事务所***
D. Wall Dramatic Treasure - ***Christian Organisation 基督徒集团***

i. Puritan Music the **Rainbow Bridge Note**
ii. Biblical Genetic Science the **Lilith & Jacob Oriental**
iii. Crime Repeated Villain the **Tither Blueprint**
iv. Mathematics **Criminology Rootcause and Historical Evolution**

v. Theology Reinvention based onto **Stellar Science, Mileage Science, Metrology Science**

Y692. Universal Duty: Eschatology Calendar define the date of Population Census (Bulletin)

Lamb non repel former false chris
lock1x100perx1000yrs=200metai.e. 10kx100k
100million person

1 person should has approx. 270meta social friend

1/16 populated is Adventist SG->MY (Modern Exodus)
Oriental is developed country fashioned society.

Adventist is God kingdom arrival. in MY's Oriental. US

Hence by Lock 3, 12 years, we can reach the 270million person populated globally.
But it could be more accounts of unpopulated either way.

The highest meta was in the eschatology era calendar.
(lock1)x100personx1000yrs, total 230 million

Present modern era has 75million 2016' by compress of time, the projection is 25minute. next day. 1 day distanced. 10 years distanced.

High meta is original RY Blood O type, the chinese. many of them. The Lamb. Righteous NATO. in Malaysia. the Nativity Israel, i.e 75% global populated. Jordan Sea Timezone JPN the Final Adventist 7th Islam Country

Y693. Universal Duty: Islam Diplomat 1st Round (Bulletin)

The Repel Lamb and Satan is against the High Quantum Proceeding. And Carrier became into Nazi the Popularism instead Pentecost. i.e. Elections Canaan Jews.

Islam Party Advocated this Flag against Canaan and Israel Wall.

Its required Satan Myth solved to proceed with High Quantum and Christmas tither account.

Exceptional case the salvation of non church goer is by seeking the Answer of Christmas and Satan Myth.

Y694. Universal Duty: Imperial Space Agency (Bulletin)

Property value index equal to 10 horse power max. bordered of time end. 13% efficient combustion engine.

Unity is 6000kw. Combustion efficient the quantum number efficient.

The etymology science

600kw 6000kw max
combustion efficient 13%
max 10 horse power

Celsius constant merge with Reynold constant when eschatology calendar watched time

High quantum number the high combustion efficient could hit as high as 2horse power to few linear times

Hence, property land boundary index has this analogy too the max of 10 horse power suit. The energy become the land property unit. and max index is energy packet modelled.

Drawing Board
3 meta 100 years,
Union Cyclic Dynamics

Y696. Universal Duty: Crime Disruption Essential, Man Made Creature Surgent and Sambal 38 Wall (Bulletin) (Bulletin)

i. 6per – **Corinthians (Pronouncing Sound like Islam Christian)** (True Love)(Jacob mRNA)/(Eve mRNA Cluster), Indigenous/Refugee
Tax, RQ/Omega, Herald, i.e. *Hebrew, the Rest Nativity, Herald Jerusalem Palace*
Alpha, Omega, Rocket (Numbers) or Tesla Car (**High Free Mileage, Sky High Terrain)**(*High Powered Engine)
Free Tax Sea, Same Fahrenheit Harmony Heritage the **Global Warming Dismiss (Wire Mesh DC-AC Adapter, Macintosh Platform 5G Biblical Villain Wall, Remastered Healing)** Timezone Body Disorder Covid-19 (Fire Lake Route) – Pearl liked Zone *Old A.D. 10000 to A.D. 1000* ***(End of Earth, Islam Noel Castle in the Sky)***
Anti God, Man Made Replica – **Oriental New Jerusalem Palace Blueprint Projection Disordering – Climate Disaster**
Adventist to Utopia – Urban (Adventist Calendar God Kingdom Arrival and Hiding)
Fasci Socialist, Luohan JPN/Apostolic Democrat, Hunter KR/Mafia Freelanced, Kingkong CN THAI (Boxing, Financial Layered Duty e.g. Medicine Psi 1/5th Duty)
Think Tank Islam Country – **East India Company AU MY-JB**

ii. 9per – **Galatians** (Agape)(Abraham DNA)/(Adam & Eve DNA Cluster), Diaspora/Hiatus
Config, Alpha/RZ, Meta, i.e. *Germanic, the Main Nativity, One Israel*
A-Z 50Deck, Ship (75% Percentile), **Solar Celsius Duty Car (High Free Loading, Mt Lake Isle)**, (Light Miller 13per Max Horse Power, Powered Commuter), Same Kelvin Joules the Flea Footage, the **Quantum Sky Wall Revival (Wire Mesh, DC-AC-DC, Router, HP platform 10G Rare Earth Wall, Cored Healing)** Tsunami/Evil Spirit Erotic Defect (Hell Route) – Supernova liked Zone *A.D. 500 to A.D. 1500* ***(End of World, Aladdin Castle in the Space)***
Anti Truelove the Berg Ski Mental Defect, Flea Land –
Economy Puritan unto Ecosystem Equilibrium, Myth Inclined – Aftermath Watched
Oriental to New Jerusalem – Metropolis (Eschatology Calendar the Laid and Risen)
ISIS Monarchy Democrat MY PN-KL/Mafia Organised MY MALACCA-JB (Gambling, Marketing Projection Duty e.g. Apostolic Celsius 100% Duty)
Scapegoat Western Country – **Neo Nazi RUS US UK MY-KL**

iii. 12per – **Titus** (Pluto)(Noel RNA)(Adam RNA Cluster), Aboriginal/Expatriate
Standby, RY/RA, Original, i.e. *Chinese, the Myth Nativity, Locked Eden Garden*

A-J Train (25% Percentile), **Reynold Car (High Free Powered, Moon River Habour)**, the (Only Shared Isle Made, *Holden Subaru Myvi, Renault), Same High Reynold Platform unto Isle Asia, the Climate Change Locked Liberal Sky – **Promised Land Abundancy of Food (Wire Mesh AC-DC Transformer, IBM platform 8G Logistic Wall, Crab platform 6G Knowledge Wall, Anthropology Healing)** Nuclear/Earth Quake (1st Resurrection Route/Express Resurrection Route) – Vivid liked Zone *B.C. 5000 to B.C. 1* ***(End of Time, Babel Tower Islam Eden Garden)***
Anti Semitic the Organic Skin, **Murdering Threat – Massacre**
Promised Land to Renaissance – **Summit (Passover Calendar Jesus 2nd Coming and Return)**
Fasci Communist ITA PHILIPPINES/Nazi Communist UKRAINE VIET/Mafia Underground INDONESIA (Dog Fight, Security Cast Out Duty e.g. Cowboy Reynold 1/4th Duty)
Stakeholder MY SG TW CN MACAO HK – **Qing Syndicate BRU INDIA ARAB MY-PN**

Y697. Universal Duty: The Creation of Four Creatures & Four Final Resort of Heaven from Begins (Bulletin)

i. **Crabmachine hybrid Platform**, Commuting instead Commuter etc. 3G recognition Time lapsed mechanism
CPU A-J Duty Free Moses, Santa Clause
Chronology Calendar, Commuting Enclosure, the **Traffic Control**
e.g. Tabernacle 3G, Chapel 4G, Cathedral 5G, Hunger Machine 6G
Salted Powered Free Loading Rocket
Best Free Rating Climate Protocol unto Carrier
Olive Earth – Heaven Inaugural
Dead End Mileage (Creamy Like Route)(Stalled Sequence Protocol, Islam Renaissance)

i. **HP regulator Platform**, Router, 10G charismatic spirit
CPU A-J Celsius Flea J-suit, Jesuit
100% security unto SOP Banking Thaad etc. Advanced Mirroring
Calligraphy Automatic Wave Correlation by Small Bytes Only, the **Mining Burner**
Free Costing High Reynold Platform Combustion
Adventist– Oriental Express
Fire Lake (Pearl Liked Route)(Stalled Series Mapping, Babel Tower)

iii. **Macintosh Scalar Platform**, Adapter, 5G standard connecting
GPU ASCII A-Z Kelvin Flea C-suit, Joshua
Highest Ranked only here, Seeking by Sniff Virginia Footage in Oriental
High End DC-AC ***Cryptography Ferrite Core***, the **Fuel Adapter**
Free Mileage Tesla Car Homogenous Free Mileage unto Psi Routing Discreet
Oriental - Renaissance
Hell (Supernova Like Route)(Stalled Generation Axis, Noel Ark)

iv. **IBM modular Platform**, Transformer, 8G climate act
APU HEX A-Z Fahrenheit Flea R-suit, James
Standard Function, Star Dust Commitment
Specific Universal Constant Corresponded Function
High Mach Logarithm Manual Control presently, ***Carrier Loading Value 3 kinds Nozzle Flame by Feedback*** Burden, Jet Turbine, Air Compressor, the **Quantum Generator/Compressor**
Carbon UV wind or Light Miller Feedback Commuter Flipflops 4per
Free Loading Rocket 12per chain reaction
Promised Land – Utopia
Inaugural to Express Resurrection (Vivid Like Route)(Stalled Rolls Mining, Eden Garden)

Y698. Universal Duty: Tax Energy Packet (Bulletin)

Loyalty corresponded Celsius Platform
Logo Vectorial Scalar

Hence, Biblical the Tither is max up to ¼. Book of Titus. 1/5 or ¼.

Beyond than that is considered frauded.
e.g. Swiss Red Cross. One tax is opposed the Orientation.
Symmetrical Logo is non tither.

And Triangular is the most tax. i.e. 1/3. Crime Duty

Odd number & Compound Tax is Non tither. Even number is God tither.

Celsius Redefined as 0-37.5 Celsius Linear 0.625 as Quartet Duty. Max.

Humour and Secular Fundamentalist '6' 8per and final resort to heaven, the wholly population.

Y699. Universal Duty: Messiah as a Fundamentalist Essential Qualification (Bulletin)

UN, the digital organisation standard is about 222 friends. Therefore, the 270 friend is mean for 30% Duty. The Crime Syndicate. What sought after and thence.

Hence, Fundamentalist is Socialist the Thinktank and defined by scaled of friends.

Reynold as high as 20% protocol the biblical standard. Book of Titus, the tither 3rd 4th->20th. The Cross tither is 4th.
To make cowboy more cowboy is lion boy.

Apostolic Duty is max 100%
Heaven Duty is max 150%:150% twins

Hence 30% duty is just wrong division of time metric.

That is sustainability profit. Crime Syndicate non important of worker or membership.

Quantum 3.
Moses Law item 3. 12.5 Weighted.

Empty tither Account.

This kind of Activities consider the Jehovah Witness Church by no means.
The Nazi of Congregational with Cross tither Parallel Account.
Empty Cross in another sense.
Practical than emotion.
As long non false Holy Spirit.

Good Tither is non frauded.

Crime Syndicate secure their Logo remark as sole harness or disruption no time.

Y700. Universal Duty: The Samuel tension the War & Wall Treasure of All Times (Bulletin)

Renaissance from Democracy to Nationalist Era

i. Repel Lamb Monarchy Suit
Abraham Generations – Cina Celebrity, Suns 太阳的后裔 (Huangpu, Mt Lake)
Imperial Agency
Samuel (Security Machine), Goat (Dragon Remarks Whitelist)
TW, Olive Pineapple Economic Belt, 999 Tree (Chinese Security to/from Trade)
Technology Economic Belt
IBM Climate Act i.e. Anti Tsunami (Universal Electronic Instrument)
Kelvin Mark 99%:1% not 1%:99%
DNA Chromosome Staging 8G ESD Navigation (Social Disorder White Collar Wall, Anti Semitic) – Zechariah->Habakkuk->Malachi unto Adventist Calendar

ii. Royal Traitor Democracy Suit
Noel Offspring – Germanic Warrior, Hans 汉室 (Hakka, Coral Isle)
Democracy Federal Finance
Chronicle (Queen the Royalist Medicine), Sheep
MY, Fig Tree has Leaf (NGO Freelanced to/from Gurus Governors)
Chronic skips Nerve Disease the Religion Therapy, Developed into Injection failed then Codec persistency
Crabmachine Quantum Codec Defence i.e. Anti Pandemic)(Enclosure Time Metric Machine IR Geothermal Powered Commuting)
Herald Hall Mark 100% or 40%:60% not 99.5%+0.5%
RNA Geothermal Processed Annealed Cored 5G IR powered (Marriage Defect Wall, Anti Christ) – Nehemiah->Ezra->Ether unto Eschatology Calendar

iii. Cell Schism Republican Suit
Jacob Cultured – Tiong Hua Hero, Chus 楚国 (Shuzhou, Moon River Habour)
Gross Schism the Vatican, Fasci Socialist Thinktank Luohan #19 God Father
Ruth (Fundamentalist), Sigma (Blacklist)
SG, Canyon Road Uniforms Duty, Olive Durian, (Agency Professional to/from Labour Workforce)
Economic Commuter
HP Totalitarianism Ionised, from Time to Traffic Control i.e. Anti Terrorism (Android Workstation Facelift EMF Feedback Mining)
Hall Mark 60%:40% not 95.5%+4%+0.5%
mRNA 10G UV Codec (Weapon Replica Wall, Anti God) -Jobs->Chronicle->Ruth->Samuel->Kings->Judges unto Family Union Calendar

iv. Cell Schism Democrat Suit
Jacob Viral – Manchu Lotus, Royal 诸侯 (Hokkien, Sky High Tower)
Deficit Schism the Bluehouse Nationalist Socialist
Judges (Messiah), Lamb
HK Schism Road 666 Tree, Fig Tree hasn't had Leaf (Church Goer to/from MNC Head Hunter Classified)
'64' Events Crabs
Macintosh Connectivity Geothermal Manipulation i.e. Anti Earth Quake (Apple Mobile Generations ESD Motorised Jet Loading)
Data Mark 75%:75% not 50%:50%
DNA Cluster 6G EMF Conceived (Christian Persecution Wall, Anti Chinese) - Exodus->Deutonomy->Numbers->Leviticus->Genesis unto Passover Calendar

Herald Church the Charismatic & Islam Jihad Stellar Head, the One & Only Spiritual Leader Pyramid

The Civil War Wall is on Blueprint Crime Disruption

TW & CN tensions arose and arise on Blueprint Wall the Crime Disruption Treasure as for current, Mexico Wall & Strait Wall.
The Famous HP platform vs Mac Platform
High Capita but low Meta Biblical Villain makes
3 Sigma and 666 **i.e. 1per 100% meta**

Errata 19Apr2023

Y701. Universal Duty: Troubleshooting the 4 Kind of Computer Platform (Bulletin)

Universal Instrument

i. HP Connectivity Processed Wall has to be no filtered. Low Class. Robotic IoT machine. Transportation Commuter Rejection accessed is crime conspiracy lead to Guinea Colony. the Corruption Immigration Issue escalating. Lead to Pandemic outrage. “Free Immigration Museums” Sea Federation

ii. Macintosh Audio Processed Wall has to be transparent Monitoring. Semiconductor Manufacturing Access to security in no time. Rejection is desirable due Highly Ranked Security Machine.
“Free Tollzone” Land Road

iii. IBM Graphic Processed Wall has to be High filtered. Most High ranked. Airport Highly Custom Filtered Immigration of Air Traffic Control. Prevent Pandemic. No issue up to now.
“Weather Free” Airport Tower

Volume 2: Ecosystem Sky Hue

For Sheep only the Natalie

优生主义

Y636. Doctrinal Training: Final Findings of Alpha End Loops to Herald End Loops to Inaugural or Omega End Loops (Census)

Figure 2 CHI RHO CROSS

I. Industrial Evolution Framework – Utopia the Generations of Democracy Sins the Word Prison Route Silkroad
Part A. Space Science the Exodus
Solar Calendar – Opera – Train, Bus – Evening, Geneva Axis 12 Clan 莫待无花空折枝
Comet Calendar – Explorer – Rocket, Car – Six Season, Tropical Axis 6 Clan 8.1 Cyclic 百尺竿头更进一步
Lunar Calendar – Fire Fox – Ship, Aircraft – Dusk, Cancer Axis 9 Clan 孔雀东南飞, 候鸟向南飞
Sow: Etytology Chronicle
Rip: Book of Life, Ruth

Part B. Universal Machine the Unicorn – Promised Land the 8th Generations Unicorn, Quantum 8fold, 6.25Nano Scaled Metric
4.1 Engine: Metro, Chrono, Navigation, Commuting, Commuter
10.1 Mechanism Compressor : Linkage, Bearing, Transducer
Sow: Etytology Samuel
Rip: Book of Life, Job

Continue on Next Page

Continued

II. Medicine Evolution Framework – Renaissance the Rolls of Mortar Sins the Colony Route Canyon Mile End

Part A. Biblical Genetic Science the Canonical of 9 Generic Communities
Adam->Eve the Ribs and Gel liked – Genesis
Conceived Chronography – RNA the EMF Stellar i.e. Nano Scaled Organism – Organic liked
Abraham->Sarah the Pharasee – Exodus
Chromosome Navigation – DNA Cluster the ESD Motorised i.e. Energy Packets – Gel liked
Noel->Sigma the Canaan – Deutonomy
Viral Jumper Metrology – mmDNA the IR Residue i.e. Fruity – Dust liked
Jacob->Lilith the Unicorn – Leviticus
Sow: Etytology Kings
Rip: Book of Life, Poetry

Part B. Medicine Category Department – Oriental Renaissance the Part I, II the 27 Real Value, Discreet Footage Clan to Linear Footprint Clan
RNA Route to Oncology – Generic to A to Z, i.e. General Organ Acute Failure, to Multiple Enzyme of 3 layer the Specific Tailored Medicine Remedy for Organic liked
DNA Route to Nerve Chronic – Vitamin refer to Chemistry Bulletin i.e. Nutritous Herbs for Gel Liked
mmDNA Route to Viral Disease – Quantum Fabric Treament i.e. Physiotherapy for Dust liked
Sow: Etytology Judges
Rip: Book of Life, Proverb

Continue on Next Page

Copyright (C) 2023, Ryan Lai Hin Wai, All Right Reserved

Continued

III. Hollywood Action cum Drama Framework – Adventist the Inaugural Lead the Oriental Fig Tree the Pineapple Road (*Whenever has Leaf)
Part A. Crime Disruption Foundation cum
Synaetic Gospel Canonical
Zechariah Suit – Lock 10, Everyyear 1 Suit
Climate Protocol – Leviticus
Hygienic Policy – Adam the Jude
Nuclear Treaty – Canaan
Malachi Suit – Lock 6, 31st Dec every year
Global Warming the Carrier, Economic Congress war – Hebrew, Fasci 14 Walls, Matthew Gospel the Christmas Tither
Quantum Weapon the Sky, Library Knowledge war – Jewish, Marxism 7 Walls, Mark Gospel the Flowers Treasure
Meta Fallency, the Man Made Wildfire war – Israelite, Nazi 16 Walls, John Gospel the Mariology Meta Merge
Final Wall is 2023' Dec 31'st, 3rd Jan 2024' to Resurrection.
Sow: *Ecumenical Judification*
Rip: *Revelation Heaven Boundary Distance*

Part B. Marriage Doctrine & Dogma – 7th Heaven the Pearl Route
New Testament Canonical
Philemon vs Colossians: Meta Fade 75:75 (Final Freed, Official) Heaven the Real one 7Up
Titus vs Judea: Meta Growth 60:40 (Hit Cup to Last Resort, Sealed) Lent & Wall to Family & Marriage
Galatians vs James: Meta Split 50:50 (Consecutive Striked, Signature) Economic Treasure
Corinthians vs Hebrew: Meta Merge 99:1 (Memorandum, Flagship) Hygienic & Justice
Sow: *Eschatology Calendar of Sambals*
Rip: *12 Fruits of Tree*

Y638. Doctrinal Training: Dogma Law, in which yield the Protocol of Misconduction of Love or Marriage Duty (Census)

i. Artistic Love 96/Mentor Love 73 Sotong UFO Refugee Meta Fade Flash Light
Natalism vs Cranberries/Hatred
Hatred Love
Ancient Dragon – Intellects (High Meta, Official)
Sealed Heritage Fade into Wrong Hands

ii. Agape 86/Liberal Love 66 Dust Renaissance Rabbit Pie Meta Split Threat White light
Bridgate/Playboy vs Zombie
Triangle Love
Black Dragon – Mafia (Low Meta, Stakeholder)
Marshall False Love
Inheritance of Sealed Heritage

iii. Pluto Love 68/Romance 69 Organic Tiger Pharisee Meta Growth Gland light
Scout vs Linger/Love Triangle
iv. True Love 37/Holiness Love 99 Unicorn Wisdom Meta Merge Polar Light
Commuting/Pharisee vs Penthouse/Pink Panther
Mummy Love – Apostolic/Presidential
Dark Dragon/White Dragon – Freelance (High Gross Exchange per Capita, Thinker *Street Fighter & Strait Wall)/Governor (High Groos Exchange Capital, Doer)
Brothehood Robinhood False love
Meta Merge of 7 Sealed

Y639. Doctrinal Training: Canonical Illustration, The Scheme, Vision, Goal and Mission setting of Christian Agency (Census)

i. **John Gospel:** Property Value in terms of Meta the Currency Treasure.
Acts: St Joseph Stevenberg Foundation Patrick Foundation
Jesus as Godness/Angel/Paralysis
Advent – Love or Marriage Duty
Bureau License Intellectual the Heritage Lawsuit
Discipleship to Sainthood - Harvest Pentecostal to Charismatic Church, Congregational 琼瑶三毛
Pentecost Hall Mark Achievement Sealed Vision, e.g. Publish Workstation, Portfolio Studio

ii. **Matthew Gospel:** Economy Treasure in terms of Gross Schism.
Acts: St Paul Michael Hunter Rabbi Cupid
Jesus as King/Prophet/Bankruptcy
Oriental – Crime Disruption & Carrier Commuting
Intelligence Credential Economic the Marriage Sanction
Apostolic - Wesley Methodist Fundamentalist Church, Anglican 卫斯理霍金
Metric Standard Quantum Flagship Goal, e.g. Space Agency, Genetic Agency

iii. **Mark Gospel:** Crime Disruption Blueprint in terms of Pentecost, Holoscopic, Holysee.
Jesus as Servant/President/Desperado
Renaissance – Medicine Democracy to Royal Medicine (*Not Medicine Royalism)
Testimonial Witnesses Marriage Scheme the Accusement Channel

iv. **Luke Gospel:** Technology to Medicine Coring Evolution in terms of Allergy to Preliminary Platform
Acts: St Peter Peter Cupid Peterburg Hunter
Jesus as Unicorn/Genius/PhD
Utopia – Mathematical Mining to Scientific Exploring and Theology Multiplying
Identity Certificate Criminal the Quarantine Treaty
Preacher - Kindness Presbyterian Catholic Church, Vatican 金庸刘墉
Biblical Genetic Signature Mission, e.g. Security Manufacturing Issued, Security Financial Issued

Y646. Doctrinal Training: Venue, Technology, & Methodology to Christian Affiliated Nativity Salvation (Census)

i. High Meta HK vs Fig Tree, JB (Asteroid/Comet vs Land, Holoscopic->Parametric), Kelvin Mark
Alternated Core: Stakeholder (Moon Calendar – Conspiracy Activity)
3G GSM, KRE vs DPRK (Love or Marriage Duty Capital)(Great China the Pearl Wall, SilkRoad the Guinea Wall, Berlin the Schism Wall, Mexico the Monarchy Democrats Wall)
Geneva Timezone vs Jordan Timezone (Desperado), 9per Clan (Myth, Rush Hour 99%:1%), 5000:1, 3 Year
as Emptiness Dream: Dramatic World
Endervour Sovereign: Apollo/Transformer (Modular->Universal)(Mono->Partial Theism)

Easter: Flagship (Zombie), Arminianism Theology - Socialism cum Communism, Messi & Nazareth the Scout 弥撒与哪吒勒 (Rohs De-viral)

Habakkut Day: Flagship (Trojan Horse), Mariology Theology - Socialism cum Communism, Messi & Nazareth the Bridgates 弥撒与哪吒勒 (Rohs De-viral)

The Inaugural Feeling Fig Tree: Mile End the Airport Promised Land – 200 Meta Union Clans (Trains), the Oriental Express

ii. High Capital TW vs Olive, PN (Moon/Sky High vs Sea, Orthogonal->Aerial), Hall Mark
Extra Core: Doer (Comet Calendar – Massacre Activity)
4G LTE, CN vs HAWAII (War & Wall Treasure)(Israel Wall the Revival)
Moscow Timezone vs Bethlehem Timezone (Tither Account Christian), 12per Clan (Certification, Watched Day 1:10), 300:1, 2 Year
as Day Dream: Spiritual World
Perseverance Sovereign: Chang'er/Iron Man (Scalar->Commuter)(Partial->Monotheism)

Christmas: Official (Lion Face Human Body), Calvinism Theology – Commonwealth, James/Joshua/Santa Claus

Passover Day: Signature (Linger), Christology Theology cum Vision Theology - Federal Capitalism, Chris the Salvation Army 救世军 (Lent free Exodus)

The 8th Rotten Olive: Julian the Miracle Oriental – 6 Meta Family Generic AtoZ Modern Foundations, (Rockets), the Apollo

iii. High Capita SG vs Star Dust, KL (Mars/Solar vs Sky, Pentecost->Holy See), Data Mark

Graded Core: Thinker (Solar Calendar – Crime Activities)(Strait Wall the Currency War)
5G CDMDA (2.4G the Route), JPN vs SHG, (Crime Disruption Economic Skew Currency)
Jerusalem Timezone vs Galilea Timezone (Apostolic), 6per Clan (Memorandum, Stalled Time 1:100), 24:1, 0.5 year
as Daunt Dream: Realism World
Liberal Sovereign: Wisery/Crabmachine (Enclosure->Commuting) (Trinity->Multi Theism)

Pentecostal Day: Nil Sealed (Cranberries), Victory Theology cum Anabaptism Theology, i.e. Federation Capitalism, Layla the Fundamentalist 魔鬼党 (New Jerusalem, Holy Spirit Conceived)

Halloween: Sealed (Cranberries), Advent Theology cum Canonical Theology, i.e. Federation Capitalism, Jesuit the Catholic 耶稣党 (Oz of Wizard, Spiritual Incarnation)

Y647. Doctrinal Training: Rightyard 无间道, Currency Framework, from Gross Interest Savings, Currency Issued Loans to Free Premiuer Transactions (Census)

i. Gross: Bank Polarised Light, Lock Zone - Footprint, Chipsets the Dime i.e. Paper - Orthogonal 10per Own Business, CP Egg rating
Adventist Terminal
Catholic Wons
Organised Mafia: Dragon the Remarks Stakeholder MY->KRE
Biblical Villain: Sheppard Dog the Sigma #1,2,6, #3
World War: Fighting Policy for Dramatic Heritage
22-1=20 Meta: 99:1 6per Memorandum
Meta Split (high per capita): Hygienic Recovery the Worst Rival

ii. Deficit: Loan White Light, Catch Zone - Footage, Issued Currency the Bond i.e. Cash - Holy See 8per Bank Rolls Gazing, CAPPED Layla rating
Oriental Terminal
Vatican Cents
Mafia: Freelance ThinkTank the Sheppard Dog, JPN->SG
Biblical Villain: Gentile the Unicorn Offspring, Sigma #4
Civil War: Dog Fight Protocol for Blueprint Treasure
6+6=12 Meta: 50:50 12per Ante
Meta Fade (gross capital): Preliminary Platform the Nominal Lover

iii. Exchange: Trade Rainbow Light, Free Zone - Footwell, Crime Disruption Security the Token i.e. Capita - Pentecost 5per feeling, PC Snowman rating
Promised Land Terminal
Episcopal Bytes
Whitelist Celebrity
Neo Nazi: Politician Sigma (meta +5min, Camel) the Scapegoat MACAO->US
Biblical Villain: Lost & Sheep the Repel Lamb, Sigma #5
Lambda Dust the Chinese #3 Pekinese Devil (Meta -5min, Crocodile)(Archimedes),
'#9' Gothic False Christ (Meta 25min)(Einstein, Intel), #13 Spanish False Prophet (Newton)(meta +35min, Ikea)(Black Dragon Stellar Head vs Ancient Dragon)
Cold War: Adventure & Lent Treaty the Wall
200+100=300 Meta: 40:60 Pluto:romance 9per Myth
Meta Merge (high Meta): Allergy Aggregates the Moderated Enemy Stellarhood

Errata 4Apr2023

Y648. Doctrinal Training: Chinese Dragon 中华英雄，Carrier, Marriage to Family corresponding to Blueprint Treasure the Economy in terms of Heritage (Census)

i. Husband/Wife: White Light (**Reflection RQ**)->Anabaptism Theology->Footprint Meta Number Lambda #9->Cast out – Agape Love vs Lent Love to Data Mark Footprint
Carrier->Mother: Warm Light->Vision Theology/Salvation Theology->cum Pa Rolls->**Omega Inaugural** (Doer)
Oriental - Chancellor, Surgent
Heritage the Dramatic Policy (*Hygienic of Arbitary, Bias*)

ii. Wife/Husband: Polarised Light (**Reflection Alpha**)->Victory Theology->Footwell Quantum Number Sigma #4->Layer upto – True Love vs Puppy Love to Kelvin Mark Footwell
Carrier->Father: Gland Light->Advent Theology/Canonical Theology->cum Psi Rolls->**RY Original** (Thinker)
Adventist – Private, Commander
Blueprint Treasure the Marriage Duty Protocol (*Law of Bytes, Charvin*)

iii. Wife/Husband: Rainbow Light (**Refraction RY**)->Calvinism Theology->Footage Pentecost Number Theta #16->Projection within – Pluto Love vs Romance Love to Hall Mark Footage
Carrier->Sister/Brother: Flash Light->Mariology Theology/Christology->cum Pi Rolls->**Alpha Coherent** (Stakeholder)
Promised – Colonel
Economic Wall the Lent Treaty (*Habakkuk of Love, Income*)

A. Private (Samuel, Etymology, Utopia) - Church
B. Chancellor (Chronicle, Eucharistic Doctrine, Promised Land) - Library
C. Colonel (Dragon, Eschatology Calendar, Adventist) - University
D. Commander (Kings, Ecumenical, Oriental) - Laboratory
E. Surgent (Judges, Eucharistic Dogma, Renaissance) – Office

Carrier Loading = Clay+Rib **Cost Value Interval**
Man = Clay Sigma #666->#6 total per Max Capita Value
Woman= Soft Rib/Rib Eye = Schematic Meta Lock/Dating Pentecost Lock
Carrier Commuting = Dogma+Doctrine Protocol **Cost Value Interval**

Y649. Doctrinal Training: Canonical Lawsets i.e. Ecumenical (Census)

i. **Heaven:** (Nuclear Treaty, Gel Sheep)
Nehemiah Zechariah - Coherent RQ – **Ancient Salary** (Aboriginal vs Dragon) - Chronicle, Kings, Samuel, Judges, Ruth (Occurrence)

ii. **Oriental:** (Hygienic Policy, Ashed Organic Goat)
Ether Malachi - Inaugural RA - **Anti God Compensation** (Refugee vs Sigma) - Genesis Meta, Gospels Synaetic, New Testament Etymology, Revelation Eucharistic, Exodus Eschatology Calendar (Carrier)

iii. **Adventist:** (Climate Protocol, Inked Lamb)
Ezra Habakkuk - Inaugural RZ - **Anti Christ Wage** (Diaspora vs Unicorn) - Job, Proverbs, Poetry, Deutonomy, Leviticus (Burden)

iv. **Promised Land: Heaven Bridges**
Alpha R1 - **Ancestry**
(Schism)

v. **Renaissance: Oriental Bridges**
Omega R10 – **New Generation**
(Micro)

vi. **Utopia: Promised Land Bridges**
Original RY – **Semitic**
(Trajectory)

Errata 4Apr2023

Y651. Doctrinal Training: Gentile Sky vs Global Sky vs Heaven Sky (Census)

i. **Adventist:** – Mars – Pentecost 5D (Motive, Music), Holysee 8D (Moron, Health)
ii. **Oriental:** – Moon – Holoscopic (Moral, Economy) 6D, Scenic 7D (Colour, Skill)
iii. **Promised Land:** – Sea – Orthogonal (Social, Engineering) 10D, Aerial 9D (Earth, Social)
8beats good vulnerability, rock (quartet) 4D/Pop 9D effect/sentimental 8D tones/folks 1D live **-off beat 1,2,3**
16beats evil vulnerability, jazz (hill) 7D/rock&roll 6D/opera/bassa nova/**-off beat 1,2,3**

Y655. Doctrinal Training: Heaven, Earth and River, Sea Made (Census)

The 2 Kind Venue of Star Dust, Clay or Mined: Alpha Adventist or Omega Adventist – 20 Meta Chronicle Church, 2 Original Leader Suit (Ships), the Rainbow Bridge
*1 Meta = equivalent to all of these, not the least about 1:12500 populated
i. 99% 1% Graded Bonding i.e. Meta Montage, Pyramid in 6->3 Rolls (5000per Max to yield equilibrium), Office (God the Independent Anointed, Salary)
Organic - Earth Made
Monotheism - Adventist
ii. 99.5% 0.5% Graded Bonding i.e. Meta Montage, Cube in 6->2 Rolls (7500per Max to yield equilibrium), Church (Independent Cultivated, Award)
Protein a.k.a. Rib Eye, the Sea Made Schematic
Multitheism (Mary Says Dominancy) - Oriental
iii. 50% 50% Shipping Enclosure i.e. Etymology Calibre, Boat in 12->2 Series (AtoZ, 1351per, Quartet Populated), Clan (Christian the Natalie Atonement, Wage)
Gel a.k.a. Soft Rib Heaven Made
Trinit-ism (False Christ Villain) – Promised Land
iv. 40% 60% Quantum 3 i.e. Devotion, Bridge in 9->6 Era (5% Laplace Loss), 36+2C+2R/43 Prism Refraction Degree (Rainbow Bridge Salvation the Exclusive), Foundations (Public the Exchanged Redemption, Compensations), Twister 100% Meta 12500per ~Loss 625per Rainbow Bridge Meta
Dust - River Made
Partial-theism (Nazareth Salvation) – Utopia

Y656. Doctrinal Training: J-suit Interstellar End Time Note (Census)

J-suit. NATO: Fighting: i.e. Atonement by Duty Protocol: Fire Lake Route->Mt Lake (New High)
Harbour: Moon River Dust #10 Johor Strait/Lido
Abraham: 杭州 壮族/闽南 (RY), Thinker
Pineapple Oriental Olive A-Z, Spiderwoman
Adventist – Lost & Found Sheep
Lock 10: Immediately, Passover Day 逾越节, Adam Road (-5min)

I-suit. Vatican: Marty i.e. Redemption by Duty Protocol: Heaven Route->Christmas Herald
Harbour: Clay Dust #9 Sentosa/Pontian
Adam: 南京 琼族/荆州 (Alpha), Stakeholder
Mint Olive A-J, Chang'er
Oriental – Repel Lamb
Lock 9: Last Day, New Year Eve Day 末日节, Nazareth Metropolis (-1min)

H-suit. NASA: Sacrifice: Eternal Life Route->Abundancy Life
Harbour: Seafood Dust #8 Sembawang/Stulang
Noel: 黄埔 汉族/满族 (RQ), Celebrity
Fig Tree I,II,III,IV, Monalisa
Promised Land – Sheppard Dog
Lock 8: Inaugural day, i.e. First of May 生死日 the Labour Day, Judi Force (-6min)

G-suit. FBI: Gun Lock
Harbour: Pearl Dust #1 Jurong/Iskandar
Jacob: 苏州 澳 (Omega, 50%50%), Doer
Lily 6per, Lilith Angel
Utopia Original – Anti Christ
Lock 7: Leap Year, Sport 竞技日 Competition Day, Jerusalem Laboratory (+1min)

F-suit. WHO: Disease Lock
Harbour: Pearl Dust #1 Jurong/Iskandar
Jacob: 苏州 鹤 (Omega, 40%60%), Doer
Coffee Bean 6per, Transformer Universal Modular
Renaissance Original – Dragon
Lock 6: Every 31st. Good Friday 受难日, Schism Road (-1min)

E-suit. WWF: Natural Lock
Harbour: Pearl Dust #1 Jurong/Iskandar
Jacob: 苏州 粤 (Omega, 99%1%), Doer
Orchid 6per, Crabmachine Enclosure Scalar
Renaissance Original – Unicorn
Lock 5: Next day, 25min, Easter Day 圣灵日, Jordan River, Salted Dust (+6min)

D-suit. UN: Vegetable Lock
Harbour: Pearl Dust #1 Jurong/Iskandar
Jacob: 苏州 梅 (Omega, 1%99%), Doer
Chrysanthemum 6per, Iron Man Regulator
Utopia Final – Dragon Offspring
Lock 4: Good day, Christmas Day 圣诞节, Fig Tree Road, Bethlehem Town (+5min)

C-suit. KMT: Sudden Lock
Harbour: Pearl Dust #1 Jurong/Iskandar
Jacob: 苏州 桂 (Omega, 60%60%), Doer
Sakura 6per, Commuter Compressor
Renaissance Final – Unicorn Offspring
Lock 3: Pentecost Day 升天日, Galilee Sea, Mile End Road (-6min)

B-suit. CIA: Suicide Lock
Harbour: Pearl Dust #1 Jurong/Iskandar
Jacob: 苏州 津 (Omega, 60%40%), Doer
Lotus 6per, Commuting Circuit
Renaissance Beta – Gentile
Lock 2: Seasonal, Habakkuk Day 光明日, Canyon Road (+6min)

A-suit. ZION: Hell Lock
Harbour: Pearl Dust #1 Jurong/Iskandar
Sarah: 苏州 福 (Omega, 50%50%), Doer
Sea Grass 6per, Robotic Arm
Utopia Beta – Lamb
Lock 1: Every Year, Halloween Day 复活日, Jerusalem Marketplace (+1min)

*AtoJ 10per Meta"

Celsius 0-37.5 (Dust liked), (PC rating: Low per Capita)

*Chronicles Era constituted by All Three Consecutive Clans i.e. Harmony Meta. One Chronicle equivalent to 3 Persons of Kings/Queens"

Y657. Doctrinal Training: Chronic Liver Failure, Brain Stroke and High Blood Pressure Rootcause linked to Temperature Scaling a.k.a. Climate Change (Census)

Story has no end until the begin of eternal life. Hence, the proof of Christianity is proof of God. We can thence know the Darwin is viable too. For every life has its Creator, and these Creator is creature too, so called Machine the Herald Era.

The invention of Crabmachine concept was initiate with this, the Crabmachine is anyone God within the anyone House. Whereafter the Transformer the Modular Universal Machine is anyone God within the anyone Car. There is Iron Man Machine Regulator with anyone God within the anyone Compressor Machine.

The Making of Hybrid Machine comes possible, by wire connect or wireless. I have the discreet telling all relevant governor that the Quantum weapon we suffer is just pure victory against the Viral Codec of Mindset the series. Just double action reserved by All Right Reserved of enemy of human.

USA is Scaled Dimension, AU is Community Spirit, and UK is Security Spirit Hunter. The corresponding to USA Hormone Bill, AU Carbon Oxygen Bill and UK Nicotine Bill, by delivery of Chipsets the illegally traffic.

What had risking is those without these becoming, and when these threshold less becoming to MY the Gas toxic, becoming to SG the hormone liver failure, and becoming to TW the Brain Stroke.

Thence, against of Climate is against everything, and more and more toward heaven.

Western Country VS Asia Country, the Christ Town vs George Town Wireless only vs Wired only 5G equivalent vs 10G equivalent 1G as Closure of Locked.

The Lack of Mining Material, Western becoming Nicotine Bill + Carbon Bill + Hormone Bill Kidney Failure + Gas toxic + Aged Lock tumour The Asia opposite e.g. MY_HG->SG_NC (Products)

Errata 27Mar21023

Y659. Christian Medicine XXXI: Covid-19 & Wireless Weapon Defence & Wired Automated Building Enclosure System Framework (Journal)

i. Adventist US/AU **Wireless** ***George Town, Gross high capital*** **Multinational** (2 storey, anti codec, Cancered, Bomb Threat)

ii. Oriental SHA/MCA **Wired China Town i.e. Christ Town, Low Capital Federation** (1 storey, anti chronic, Kidney Stroke, Evil Spirit)

iii. Promise Land TW/SG **Wired Night Market Town i.e. Christ Town, high per capita** (1 storey, anti chronic, Lung Toxic, Heat Tasked)

iv. Utopia GER/KR **Wireless** ***Funky Town*** **low per capita** (2 storey, anti codec, Disease, Gas Toxic Threat)

v. Renaissance MY/EU **Wireless/Wired (None of Both Active for Distorted Malfunction)** ***Christ Town, Federal Gross Capital*** (3 storey, anti rolls the Distorted Ether Protein, Geothermal Tasked, Foreign Gene)

vi. Eden Garden HK/US **Wireless IT Mall Town i.e. Isle Town, Federation Gross Capital** (2 storey, anti codec, Nerve Failure, Wireless Halted Threat)

*Quantum Skew cause Organ Disorder Disease Codec e.g. Covid-19 related Pandemic the low per capita Disease.

Y658. Doctrinal Training: Samuel Suit the Non Weapon Technologist of Singapore Inventions (Census)

Wireless the Quantum Connection vs Wire the Gridded Connection
4.9G vs 10.1G
5G Ionised Wave vs 10G Seismic Wave Geothermal Shortage of Ionised becoming Radiate Shortage become into worsen Climate Change

Shortage of Radiation become improved Climate Change.
Usage of e.g. SSD Cold Material tend inclined into improving Climate.

Hall Room Involve the Geothermal ranking of 2per layer or 3per layer which deviate the division the latter into harmless Heat Turbulent of Ether Shrinking, and Harmful Heat Laminar Ether Skew.

Big Hall Room equivalent to Small Enclosure the Reverb, Cubicle Hall Room is equivalent Big Enclosure the Echo.

The knowhow this yield the Wireless and Wired usage. Biased the Wired Could just solved the Climate Change the think out of the box.

Y668. Doctrinal Training: Automated Heaven least the Legislation Attorney, Covenant Atonement, Rituals Redemption (Census)

i. **Certified Rituals Redemption** (2nd Coming Jesus)
Eschatology Calendar & Judification->12 Fruits of Genealogy->World War

(Corinthians & Ruth **20per Alpha-Omega** (Rainbow Bridges), Princess Meta (99%1%) Sealed vs

20 Chronicle Kings & Judges **500per meta (12500person)**, Generic Top 25% percentile the Harmony Ship (Titus Ship), Gentile Meta (50%50%) Signature vs

Samuel & Jobs **5000per A-J** (Concept Car) (40&60%) Original Meta Flagship) (Oriental->Castle in the Sky)

ii. **License Covenant Atonement** (Jesuit i.e. J-suit Christ)
Ecumenical Lawsets->Canonical Apostolic Church->Cold War (Sigma vs Lambda, Epsilon)(Adventist->Star War)

iii. **Treaty Collector** (Messi i.e. Merciful Christ)
Eucharistic Congress->20 ranks Economic Kingdom->Civil War (16 Dust vs 14 Organic)(Promised Land)

iv. **Legislation Attorney** (Chris i.e. Salvator Christ)
Etymology Naming System->Book of Life->Racial Riot (Goat vs Sheep v Lamb)(Utopia<>Renaissance)

Errata 4Apr2023

Y669. Doctrinal Training: From Motive to Final Milestone (Beta+Alpha+Theta) based on Tempered Mileage, Annealed Endervour, and Pasteurised Coring (Census)

i. Herald Christmas: Germany (Presbyterian) – Oriental (Alpha Heaven, Ecumenical Lawsets)

ii. White Christmas: France (Fundamentalist) – Adventist (Original Heaven, Etymology Name System)

iii. Bethlehem Christmas: Israel (Puritan) – Promised Land (Herald Heaven, Eucharistic Judges Congress)

iv. Rest Nativity Christmas: Greece (Eastern Orthodox) – Utopia (Final Heaven, Eschatology Calendar Judification)

*New Theology called Adventist Theology more than Advent Theology

*Heaven constitutes one original Pillar 1st tier and multiple pillar i.e. the 2 tier. i.e. 7th Story Heaven or 11th Omega Heaven.

*Highlight one alternate Pillar and multiple pillar axis on main alternate Pillar is for Twin Galaxy a.k.a. Heaven Footage' Eden Garden.

*38 Sambals River i.e. Famous Croyals River – Rainbow Bridge, Titus Ship, Concept Car (i.e. since 1930s Singapore-Malaysia Strait, 1st Moon River comparable to United Kingdom and Japan Imperial)

e.g. 八仙过海，猛龙过江，双城故事

*68 Offbeat Sambals Bridge a.k.a. the Rainbow 6 Bridge. – 2nd Connection Bridge to Castle in the Sky (i.e. 5G Clan) e.g. Famous Cable Car.

*If and only the Chronicle rule out all War & Wall, the Rainbow 6 Bridge may chartered.

Y670. Doctrinal Training: 3 pico a.k.a. three universe villain (Census)

1st Generations: Ancient dragon, Pussy Cat Route (Signature, Meta Cropped, Identity Thief) - **Adventist** = Castle in the Sky

2nd Generations: Joker, Unicorn Route (Official, Natalie Guinea, Colony) - **Oriental** = Castle in the Space

3rd Generations: Stellarhood, Cinderella Route (Sealed, Etymology De-viral, Word Prison) - **Utopia** = Islam Eden Garden

Alternate Generations: Devil, Satan Claus Route (Flagship, Closed Tither Ransom, Trojan Horse) - **Promised Land** = Islam Noel

Elections comparison: Natalie vs Christian->Egyptian and/or Semitic->Revelation God and Adventist God

Y675. Doctrinal Training: The Brief of National Geography Conscience (Census)

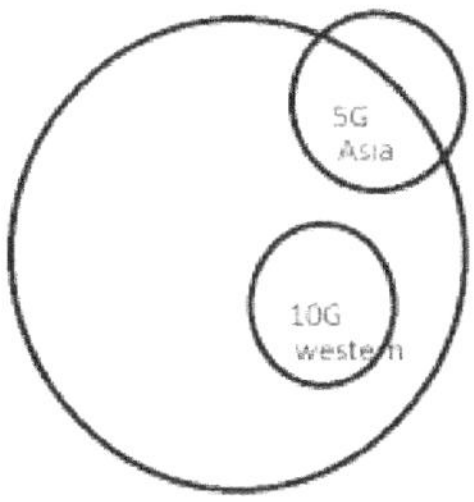

Figure 3, 5G Asia and 10G Western, Turbulent Anti Noise Enclosure and Laminar Sound Hall Enclosure Cubicle by Geneva Timezone.

i. Sky the 6per (Generations) Economy Ecosystem, Interactive Environment Hue
Resort (Orthogonal), personal, Visionary – **Gentile Meta Status (e.g. Commuting by Graphic) vs Personal Touch (Pearl)**

ii. Land the 9per (Alpha Omega) Demography 3 Benchmark Rating, Sorted Holy Spirit
Carrier (Homogenous), universal, Literacy – **Christian Identity (e.g. Commuting by Word) vs Universal Community (Evil)**

iii. Sea the 12per (Series Mapping), Geology Premium Ranking, Corresponded Human Marriage Pillar & Protocol.
Social (Holistic), regional, Operation – **Anti Christ Pentecost (e.g. Commuting by Music) vs Neighbourhood Holysee (Misconduction)**

Y676. Classification Of Ethnic IX: DNA insight & Church denominations (Bulletin)

i. **Adam (Zechariah Era e.g. World War/Cold War, Jewish 3 Sect)**
God Made (Biased): EMF Conceived, RNA Conjugates, **(Cryptography Purity Mode, Marriage Misconduction Protocol i.e. Sarah Law a.k.a. Meta Law)**(Renaissance Patriot Terrace State)
Diaspora Expatriate
Jude 朝廷皇家, 唐山 (Lost & Found Church Membership) vs Germanics 客家 (Chronicle)
Vatican Church/Methodist/Pentecostal: Pope Oriental (**UN Multinational**) – **Oriental** (Anti True Love Burden, Mafia)
Union/Chinese Union/Herald King (Wisery) – **Generic A-Z 20deck (Speed Boats) Top 75% Percentile**, **the Original R-suit**, *(Fahrenheit Harmony Natural Heaven)(Redemption Free Energy i.e. Anti Global Warming, analogy to Available Heritage)*

ii. **Abraham (Habakkuk Era e.g. United Nations/G20 Summit/World Bank, Semitic 12Sects)**
King Made (Modular): ESD Chromosome **DNA Clusters (Carrier Ranking Number, Human Right Monetary Protocol)** Navigation, (Aboriginal Isle Clans)
Canaan->Gothic Diaspora 太阳的后裔, 杭州 (Repel Army) vs Hebrew 闽南 (Kings)
Fundamentalist Church/Anglican: Nil (**UN Federation**) – **Adventist** (Anti Natalie Christian Burden, Cult)
Standard/American Standard/King James (Apollo) – A-J **(Express Train)**, **J-suit Graded Heaven** *(Lock Free Demography, analogy to Eternal Life)*

iii. **Noel (Malachi Era, e.g. Olympics/World Cup/Soccer League, Hebrew as Bottomline Natalie)**
Queen Made (Scalar): IR Powered **mDNA Cored, (Kelvin Ranking Number, Climate Protocol)**(Analogy to 38 Sambals River) (Heavenly Pentecost Mt Clan)
Levi->Jewish 明太子, 壮族 (Royal Traitor) vs Roman 潮州 (Ruth)
Episcopal Church/Presbyterian: Patrick (**UN Nationalist**) – **Promised Land** (Anti Semitic Burden, Nazi)
English Standard/New King James (Samuel) – **Alpha to Omega Chronicle Wall Treasure**, **(Free Load Rocket)**, *(Reynold and/or Celsius i.e. Apostolic and Labour Duty)(Atonement Free Food i.e. Anti Climate Change, analogy to Crime Conspiracy Retreated)*

iv. **Jacob (Adventist Era e.g. Cowboy (Canaan)/ 1st Of May (British)/Christmas (Gothic)(New Jerusalem)**
Man Made (Interposed): e.g. Music & Doctrinal Era vs Milk Powder Codec Era, **UV Viral Codec**, **(Stellar Ranking Number, Universal Time Metric Commercial Tax Protocol)**(Utopia Christ Habour)
Indigenous Refugee
Hebrew 楚国诸侯, 湘族 vs Israelite 汉室家族, 汉族 (Community Cell Schism) vs Greek 广府 (Samuel)
Catholic Church/Charismatic: Rabbi (**UN Islam Monarchy 6per Islam Prophet**) – **Eden Garden** (Anti God Made Burden, Any Jihad)
Contemporary Kings/Rohs (Ruth) – **Generic A-Z, 1 & only deck A-Z (Tesla Car), Top 25% Percentile, the Omega Liberal Heaven**, (Nil)

Y681. Doctrinal Training: The Deeper Salvation to Innocent Zombie, Mermaid & Trojan from Escalating (Census)

Commercial:

i. linkedin vs alibaba: Mafia Dragon, Scapegoat (Remarks, whitelist) vs Mafia Freelance (Foundation, networth)
ii. twitter vs instagram: Nazi Leader (Sealed, marriage) vs Neo Nazi Stakeholder (Official, network)
iii. facebook vs youtube: Islam Jihad, thinktank (Signature, logo) vs Organised (Flagship, photo)
Popularism: Pentecost->Youtube
Pentecostal: Holysee->Twitter

Religion:

i.EU buried: (Zombie): waiting Jesus return
ii. MY: puritan (Mermaid): Eden Garden, Devil (Fire Lake)
iii. AU linger: (Trojan Horse): Adventist beta to final (100 years once)
i.US (lamb,carrier) Pentecost (Passover): Gentile (Fire Lake), 1000 years
ii. UK: (goat,logo) Express Resurrection (Easter), Ancient Dragon vs Christ (1st Resurrection)
iii. RUS: (sheep,meta) 1st resurrection: (Halloween), Satan (Hell), 1000 years
71 Heaven
7th 1st Reason and Original Heaven

6 stepper rate Currency, Currency the Property of Stone, 6per to 12per Property of Scissor

UN MNC vs Federation: dollar vs aud: Oxford vs Broadway->Labour (5days) Brain cells
NATO vs Islam: won vs aud: Gross vs High Capita->Poverty (college), Life
WWF vs HK: token vs cent: Cambridge vs Legacy->Business (2days), Energy
KMT sterling vs bucks: Deficit vs Trade ->Research (master), Blood cells
NASA grand vs yuan: Harvard->Wall (holistic marketing), ROSMOS: (reverse finance), Bytes
WHO vs pound (Yeast) vs dime (Brew): Orthogonal->Treasure (replica revolution), Watched

Cultured->Ruth->Mafia, Goat vs sigma
Cultivated->Kings->Nazi, Lamb vs gentile
Insight->Samuel->Organised, Sheep vs anti christ
Christ ->Ante Lock10 Anti christ, vs Christ Habour, 3per meta cored
Ritual->by Priest vs by Montage vs by Currency
Spiritual>Dream>Realism

Y683. Doctrinal Training: 9 typical Christian Calendar for Spiritual Prayer & War (Census)

i. **Meta Calendar, Lunar Calendar->Eschatology Calendar** watched Jesus 2nd coming, lock7 Gels Conspiracy (meta clan), Halloween, White Christmas, **Gathering a.k.a. Anthropology (Immigration Meta, the Marriage Misconduction Assurance Principle i.e. Ezra Law the Calendar Correlation Justice),** Intelligence

Islam Law: Commercial Law – Business Treasure Sabotaging e.g. Mafia Technology

ii. **Weather Calendar**, Lent Day i.e. Watch Day the Rocket Dating, **Pentecostal Calendar**, **Adventist Calendar**->God Kingdom arrival->Stellar Ranking Kelvin Mark, Hall Mark, Easter Eden Garden Christmas, **Dating a.k.a. Remastered (Carrier Loading Value, Love the Lite Duty a.k.a. Carrier Duty Protocol, Corinthians Law the Communication Protocol),** Processed

Islam Law: Intelligence Law – Terrorism onto Incomplete Studied e.g. Cult Activities

iii. **Solar Calendar, Sport Events Calendar**, **Family Union Calendar (ref Book of Samuel),** Dust Criminal->Pentecost, Generations axis, Passover, Holy Night, **Fellowship a.k.a. Coring (Hall Mark the Repeated Criminal Repentance, Exodus Law the Puritan Debt Account),** Broadcast

Islam Law: Human Right Law – Capital Defect Crime e.g. High Meta Criminal

Copyright (C) 2023, Ryan Lai Hin Wai, All right reserved.

Y687. Christian Medicine XXXII: Body Cored and Timezone Disorder led Generic Heart Inflammation (Journal)

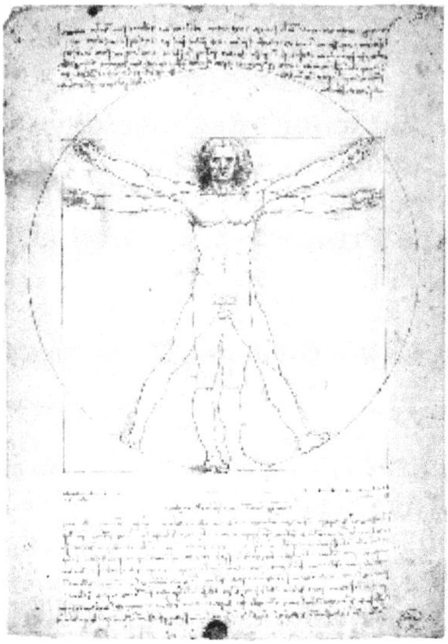

Figure 4 Da Vinci Status reflection of Geneva Timezone at the Head.
i.e. Covid-19 & Leprosy the Skin Fatal Disease

i. Ether Law
Chinese Royalism the Academy Hierarchy UN Federation->Tsunami Vulnerability
Geneva Timezone (EU to SG) - Oriental
Head to Feet->Tsunami the Meta Timezone Disorder i.e. Codec Healing 10G
Commit: Rabbi->Chancellor, Timothy (Singh) – Attorney: Rare (Ok)
Catholic (Judges, Messi)

ii. Nehemiah Law
Indian Democrat UN Federal->Genocide Vulnerability
Bethlehem Timezone (AU to SHA) - Adventist
Feet to Foot->Genocide the Toxic Gas, i.e. Codec Disruption 5G
Commit: Pope->Commander, Philemon (Hebrew) – Attorney: Elections (NG)
Herald (Samuel, David)

iii. Habakkuk Law
Jews Republican UN International->Nuclear Vulnerability
Jerusalem Timezone (TW to MY) - Renaissance
Body to Neck ->Terrorism the Time Metric High Tax i.e. Codec Blueprint Clinical 9G
Commit: Bishop->Surgent, Thessalonians (Gothic) – Attorney: High Mileage (Ok)
Puritan Music (Kings, Solomon)

iv. Ezra Law
Islam Democracy UN Multinational->Terrorism Vulnerability
Jordan River Timezone (US to JPN) - Utopia
Right Hand tips to Left Hand tips ->Nuclear the Footage Discreet i.e. Codec
RF Wave 7G
Commit: Patriarch->Colonel, Titus (Manchu) – Attorney: Trend (Ok)
Fundamentalist (Ruth, Nazareth)

Errata 15Apr2023

Y690. Silk Road: The Introduction to Holistic Science as well as Holistic Medicine. (Journal)

Light is purity.

Each light is one meta.

in its own field but with man field either.
but standalone and interactive to parallel.

Light is pure, at any junction.
The one to many, and many to one filtered is easy.

This is called chaos theory the quantum 8 cyclic
energy packet knots, you can mark down same timeline repeated.

Chaos Theory first law. equality in timeline.

Chaos Theory 2nd law. mirror and originality and coherent is discreet, in prior.

3rd Law, the total conserved of entropy is the conjugated. The index of liberal and arbitrary.

Borrow from Newton First Law, 2nd Law, and 3rd Law. The Celsius duty platform is same to Reynold Duty platform and Quantum Duty platform, Carrier Duty platform too.

Possessed this platform algorithm, all are conserved.

This can applied to many academic, industrial, theology or so.

..all the generations from Abraham to David were fourteen generations, and from David to the deportation to Babylon fourteen generations... Matthew 1:17

这样，从亚伯拉罕到大卫，共有十四代。从大卫到迁至巴比伦的时候

马太福音 1:17

Commentary: The 14 Generations is one discreet Quantum Number in Ranked.

Chaos Theory 2nd law. mirror and originality and coherent is discreet, in prior. 4/14/2023 7:14 PM

Hygience Mental Miracle Method: "Light is pure, at any junction. The one to many, and many to one filtered is easy." Applied to All area incl. WWF.

Anabaptism Method: Possessed this platform algorithm, all are conserved." Politics Democracy outcome

Stellar Rank/Nano Rank/Organic Rank: The 14 Generations is one discreet Quantum Number in Ranked.

Y680. Christian Medicine: The Perpetual Regenerative Medicine Approach, the Silk Road to Omega Heaven (Journal)

i. Holistic Spiritual->mDNA Quantum cored Remastered the Trojan Horse Generic Disease – Anti True Love

ii. Vet Vaccine->Vaccine DNA->DNA Blueprint Allergy->3 or 4 jab per SOP Chronic Disease the - Christian Persecution

iii. Royal Mental->Viral Treatment->Preliminary Platform Duty Random-> Nerve Disease - Anti Semitic Conspiracy

iv. Hunger Clinical->Codec Sound Therapy->Hormone (Dust) or Nicotine (Gels) or Lung Nozzle (Clay) Disorder
Acute Disease – Man Made Conspiracy

Volume 3: God Made Cored

For Gentile Only the Non Duty Clan

外邦人

Y599. Christian Mathematics XXIII: Computer Core Evolution to Universal Thermal Sensing Machine Evolution Framework (Whitepaper)

A. **1 core:** Cache Buffering Platform
Assembly Language to Machine Language Compiler
Cryptographer Solver of all kinds.
Calendar solver as bottleneck, Color Solver, Paragraph Solver,
For Noise Control, Toxic Pollution, Viral Pollution, Graphic Censored, Algorithm Patches.
Bios Clocking i.e. Capture to Target or Locking
Manual configuration Jumper

B. 2 core a.k.a. Dual i.e. 3in1 core: Regulator->make division for benchmark, CP Egg rating, Caesar rating, Nominal rating
Oracle Platform
IBM
Database Manipulator e.g. True Colour Machine for Individual Licenses Purchase
Digital Pentecostal e.g. Mass Media Published Platform
Switch on/off set Configurable Clicks as Auto Setting.

C. 4in1 core: Cast Out Forming Engine->Simulators for all Paper, Material, Fabric, Metallurgy, Stonage, Timbered, Glassed, Silicon.
by Enclosure of Heat Treatment as Pilot run
e.g. Staging to Routing
Macintosh

D. Vectorial Quantum = Meta Sequence e.g. 16 stage (beneficial bug)to 8 stage (error bug) Pattern
Pilot Run by Navigation of passby error or further investigation.
6 core: 7 core 8 core 9 core knot 10 core
reynold status
i.e. Computer Assisting (not Computer Aid)
Android

D. 5 core: Auto Sensing for Overclocking
Microsoft OS->Robotic Arm OS, 6 Thread Pointer, Ruby->7 Thread Holder, Prism->input conserved to output Diamond 8 Thread Cyclone, Water Oscillation Filtered
9 Thread Realism Robotic Arm, Robot Dancer,
10 Thread, Seismic Wave Sensing Mill. Reynold Feedback Disaster

16 Threat Hex number e.g. 16per of Reynold as final resort. Dust Ranking the Highest Moon River. a.k.a. Coral Strait, e.g. Red Sea the Rainbow Bridge. Metrology Function Universal e.g. Advanced Living Culture Styled for Commuting, Commuter Extension

Quantum Machine

Auto Pilot

Microsoft Platform

Crab Machine borrow from Microsoft Machine

Y600. Christian Mathematics XXIV: Quantum Unity the Conservative Law (Post)

8= 1 fire lake 1+1+2 hell, earth 2+1 heaven - Jesuit False Prophet->Jesus->*Satan ISIS Prophet WWF as bottomline

8= extra core - Jesuit False Christ->Christ ->Man of Sins

8= alternate core - Jesuit *Devil Fasci UN ->Messi->Serpent

Kelvin Mark the Social Calligraphy the Thermal Blueprint Real Value.

Climate Deviation rate was represented the True Kelvin Mark Index. Hence, approaching the good time of God kingdom Arrival, the Index gradually determined inevitability.

The Property Land Value is determined by this the either way.

However, the Hoax make this kind of illusion become a normal vision due to Many Aged & Spiritual mileage Locked to make this more evitability.

Another dispute is on the Spiritual world fade against this God Kingdom Mars (2inch 3inch 4 inch) arrival, hence the Incarnation of Spiritual become reality and resurrection of dead and creature become true.

The timeframe is capture within 1 decade once this Astronomy hoax happens. The Universe is explosive and expanding at first, then auto tuning to contracting phenomenon, due to <<Quantum Unity Conservation Law>>.

Totals are 16 sambal suit the Parallel Eden Garden Footage Milestone Suit.

1. Reynold 1time x2
2. Cowboy suit TW Grand bytes Book burns
3. Wendy suit AU sterling Slot
4. Labour 1may suit MY token Cent Slot
5. Business 13th month suit UK
6. Christmas suit EU Bucks
7. African anti cult suit US Dollar Dime Blood & Drops
8. Adventist tournament suit KR Won Weapon treaty
9. Oriental renaissance suit SG Grand footprint Photo immense

Y603. Christian Mathematics XXV: Reynold Suit to Population Consensus (Whitepaper)

Reynold Suit 16x15per=240 Traffic Protocol, i.e. Lock 5, World Bank Timezone

1. Cowboy suit TW Grand bytes Book burn (TW), Anointed & Liberal
UOB Chinese Union Investment Bank
2. Wendy suit AU sterling Slot (AU), Minimal Burden to Growth
Telecom Semitic Security Agency
3. Labour 1may suit MY token Cent Slot (MY), High Calibre with Cultivated
Maybank Federation Bank
4. Business 13th month suit UK (UK), Dramatic & Instinctive
Standard Chartered Global Class Bank
5. Christmas suit EU Bucks (EU), Sixth Sense & Feeling
Wall Street Alliant Security Agency
6. African anti cult suit US Dollar Dime Blood & Drops (US), Three Rotational Carrier
Citi Bond Agency
7. Adventist tournament suit KR Won Weapon treaty (KR), Leap Frog & Delighting
New York Trade Marketplace Security Agency
8. Oriental renaissance suit SG Grand footprint Photo immense (SG), Buffered & Endervour
Great Eastern Chinese Security Agency
9. Mary Jane Pi suit, Duty Tither 1/4 (RUS), Polarised Extreamist
Daw Jones End Mile Investment Bank
10. Uniform Force Ego, Duty Tither 3/4 (NZ), Mainstream Generic
AIA Refugee Security Agency
11. Workforce Leader, First of May Duty Tither 1/5 (HK), Speech & Foreseeable
OSBC Oversea Chinese Bond Agency
12. President CEO, Duty Tither 4/5 (IRH), Typical General
Swiss End Mile Security Bank
13. Herald Christmas suit, Duty Free Datok (CAD), Orbital Cycle
JP Morgan Semitic Investment Bank
14. Intellect anti Natalie suit, Tither 100%, Christian Extreamist (MXC), Charismatic & Axis
HSBC Tionghua Chinese Bond Agency
15. Poker suit, 24Hour Duty Tither 100%, Devout Christian (JPN), Low Capita,
Celebrity Investment Bank the World Bank, *Original Footage per Capita = Property Cost Value/Standard Deviation*

16. Mahjong Suit, 24Hour Tither 100%, Marriage Devout (THA), Population Feedback i.e. Populated, Security Bank, *Populated = Tither Account Number* Bangkok Refugee Security Bank

*Traffic Protocol: **16 Category in Hierarchy Network, each consist of 15 Pilgrim Channel. This is the Projection of Blueprint 3 Treasure of Biblical Eden Garden to Israel Wall and to Inaugural Olive Economy Belt as Best Milestone.**

Lent 1st Outer Shell Level I: Traffic Protocol of Israel Olive Wall a.k.a. Economic Belt of Israel (Jerusalem Marketplace, Toll/ Fare/Bond)

Airport/Harbour /Junction Dating Number 3: Dust Galilea Sea / Jordan River, Dust: Jewish, 8Cent

Lent 2nd Out Shell Level II: Traffic Protocol of Oriental Olive Wall a.k.a. Economic Belt of Oriental Jerusalem (Singapore-Malaysia Lido Strait (not Desaru nor Stulang), Toll/Fare/Bond)

Airport/Harbour /Junction Dating Number 5: Salted Lake / Red Sea, Dust: Hebrew, 2 Cent

Lent 3rd Outer Shell Level III: Traffic Protocol of Adventist Olive Wall a.k.a. Economic Belt of Australia (Sydney, Toll/Fare/Bond)

Airport/Harbour /Junction Dating Number 1: Nile River/Aegean Sea, Dust: Israelite, Free

(Commented by '5G' Network VIP Guest of Politics Intellect, 2023')

Errata 4Apr2023

Y606. Christian Mathematics XXVI: Lock Sky and Age Lock, the Hormone to Mileage Lock the Nerve Carbonate Exhaust (Whitepaper)

100 years 1 decade has 100 lock 1 suits.

A. Lock 1: Every Year, **Halloween Day, Jerusalem Marketplace** (+1min)
B. Lock 2: Seasonal, **Habakkuk Day, Canyon Road** (+6min)
C. Lock 3: **Pentecost Day, Galilee Sea, Mile End Road** (-6min)
D. Lock 4: Good day, **Christmas Day, Fig Tree Road, Bethlehem Town** (+5min)
E. Lock 5: Next day, 25min, **Easter Day, Jordan River, Salted Dust** (+6min)
F. Lock 6: Every 31st, **Good Friday, Schism Road,** (-1min)
G. Lock 7: Leap Year, **Sport Competition Day, Jerusalem Laboratory** (+1min)
H. Lock 8: Inaugural day, i.e. **First of May the Labour Day, Judi Force** (-6min)
I. Lock 9: Last Day, **New Year Eve Day, Nazareth Metropolis** (-1min)
J. Lock 10: Immediately, **Passover Day, Adam Road** (-5min)

***Golden Rule of 1 hours *12 years, 1 years, 1hour, 4min, Golden Rule of Temptation, 1st Resurrection/2nd Resurrection Heaven Route or 1st Dead/2nd Dead Hell Route**

Errata 15Apr2023

Y621. Christian Mathematics XXVIII: Reinvention to Orthogonal Christianity a.k.a. Rainbow Bridge Church (Whitepaper)

i. World Wall & Wall (Robinhood)
Christian Organisation Christ the Last Emperor: Stevenburg
Christian Herald Chris the Regime Repel: Peterburg
Cupid Peter
Michael Hunter

Eschatology Event *(New Jerusalem)****:*** *Apostolic, Holy See Meta Quantum (Data Mark)*
Doctrine Adventist: Calendar
Heritage i.e. Hygienic (Hymn A Corinthians, Rock Bb Galatians, Jazz B Titus, Classical F Philemon)
99% 1% (Carrier Grace), Real Constant, R (J,J)
Chronicle Treasure

ii. Cold War & Wall (Neighbourhood)
Qing Organised the Academy: Non Tither Western Security Bank
Song Dynasty the Cell Schism: Tither Account Chinese Security Bank
Chinese Abraham Olive vs Western Abraham Olive
Chinese Jewish Fig Tree vs Western Jewish Fig Tree

Ecumenical Map *(Samuel, Chronicle, Kings)****:*** *Presidential, Pentecost Quantum (Kelvin Mark)*
Economy i.e. Ministry (Modular/Scalar, Probe/Scope, Enclosure):
50% 50% (Dating Number), Aggregated Pure Integer Number, J

Catechism *(Book of Life)****:*** *Doctrine Judification Carrier vs Etymology Carrier*
Wife i.e. Dust Value Prospect – Prison Social (Rip)
Father i.e. Stone Value Net Worth – Childhood Social (Dating)
Brother i.e. Diamond Value Net Worth – Retired Social (Patch)
Sister, Dramatic, Horoscopic Meta (Sow)
Mother i.e. Dust Value Prospect – Heaven Social (Carrier)
Holy Spirit Milestone

iii. Civil War & Wall (Stellarhood)
ISIS the Jihad: Land Bonding Fund
Fasci Communist the Zion Pandemic: Japan biased Bonding Fund
Fasci Socialist the UN Genocide, Royal Traitor: Korea biased Bonding Fund

Eucharistic Identity *(12per Fruits of Tree)****:*** *Doctrine Union vs Dogma Union, a.k.a. Semitic Human Right to Gender Equality to Poverty Subsidy*
60% 40% (Metric Weighed), Conjugated Dimensionless Complex Number, i (R,R,R)
Nativity the Populated

Y615. Christian Mathematics XXVII: Scaled Tolerance & Weighted along & Scheme Class (Whitepaper)

A. Organ CP Stellar Rating
B. Piano CP Egg Rating
C. Guitar Graded Nominal rating
D. Violin Benchmark rating

i. Judge is Benchmark rating Violin Benchmark rating**.** i.e. Yes or No
Hygienic Policy
Jewish EMF RNA Adam random the indigenous generations offspring
Olive Manna the **Peanut** of Abundancy the Herald
Fig Tree beared Branches, **Rose**
Prophet Zechariah Canaan Jude Levi Bearing
Prophet Malachi Hebrew, Israelite, Jewish

ii. Ruth is Stellar rating. Organ CP Stellar Rating. i.e. Ego the Best
Climate Protocol
Hebrew, Chromosome, Abraham & Sarah diaspora offspring
Fig Tree has Leaf, **Durian**
Moon River Olive Organic **Pineapple** in Near Future, the Annealed Process for making Beer Whisky sort of kind

iii. Samuel is Same kind Gather. The Guitar Graded Nominal rating. i.e.
Origin the Best
Nuclear Treaty
Israelite Viral DNA Noel offspring the refugee of aboriginal
Fig Tree no Leaf, **Oriental Rose**
Oriental Olive **Pearl Rice** the Joseph' Returns

Y621. Christian Mathematics XXVIII: Reinvention to Orthogonal Christianity a.k.a. Rainbow Bridge Church (Whitepaper)

i. World Wall & Wall (Robinhood)
Christian Organisation Christ the Last Emperor: Stevenburg
Christian Herald Chris the Regime Repel: Peterburg
Cupid Peter
Michael Hunter

Eschatology Event *(New Jerusalem)**:** Apostolic, Holy See Meta Quantum (Data Mark)*
Doctrine Adventist: Calendar
Heritage i.e. Hygienic (Hymn A Corinthians, Rock Bb Galatians, Jazz B Titus, Classical F Philemon)
99% 1% (Carrier Grace), Real Constant, R (J,J)
Chronicle Treasure

ii. Cold War & Wall (Neighbourhood)
Qing Organised the Academy: Non Tither Western Security Bank
Song Dynasty the Cell Schism: Tither Account Chinese Security Bank
Chinese Abraham Olive vs Western Abraham Olive
Chinese Jewish Fig Tree vs Western Jewish Fig Tree

Ecumenical Map *(Samuel, Chronicle, Kings)**:** Presidential, Pentecost Quantum (Kelvin Mark)*
Economy i.e. Ministry (Modular/Scalar, Probe/Scope, Enclosure):
50% 50% (Dating Number), Aggregated Pure Integer Number, J

Catechism *(Book of Life)**:** Doctrine Judification Carrier vs Etymology Carrier*
Wife i.e. Dust Value Prospect – Prison Social (Rip)
Father i.e. Stone Value Net Worth – Childhood Social (Dating)
Brother i.e. Diamond Value Net Worth – Retired Social (Patch)
Sister, Dramatic, Horoscopic Meta (Sow)
Mother i.e. Dust Value Prospect – Heaven Social (Carrier)
Holy Spirit Milestone

iii. Civil War & Wall (Stellarhood)
ISIS the Jihad: Land Bonding Fund
Fasci Communist the Zion Pandemic: Japan biased Bonding Fund
Fasci Socialist the UN Genocide, Royal Traitor: Korea biased Bonding Fund

Eucharistic Identity *(12per Fruits of Tree)**:** Doctrine Union vs Dogma Union, a.k.a. Semitic Human Right to Gender Equality to Poverty Subsidy*
60% 40% (Metric Weighed), Conjugated Dimensionless Complex Number, i (R,R,R)
Nativity the Populated

Y622. Christian Mathematics XXIX: Wireless Equalizer, the Vulnerability Man Made Technology Should Stop (Whitepaper)

i. UV LTE CN 4G/8G **(as Spacious)**
Holoscopic Meta->**Clan Melodic Soul Blockage**
Adventist->Fire Lake Route (Gland Paralysis)
Throw Back to New Jerusalem (Terrestrial, Car Rolling, Galilli James) – Unicorn (Samuel/Judges)
Plane X-Z (Cowboy Suit), Corinthians (Strait Wall), Strait Times

ii. EMF CDMA JPN 3.5G/7.5G **(as Landed)**
Orthogonal Quantum->**Trueself Lyrics Spirit Blockage**
Oriental->Hell Route (Supernova Jail)
Express to Adventist (Hill, Air Bus Mapping, Mt. Sinai Elijah) – Dragon (Chronicle/Revelation)
Extra Axis Z (Wendy Suit), Hebrew (Florida Wall), Epoch Times

iii. ION EDGE MY 7G **(as Lent)**
Promised Land->2nd Resurrection to Utopia Route
Departure to Oriental (Coral Isle, Bus Remastering, Exodus) – Sheppard Dog (Kings/Ether)
Alternate Axis Y (Labour Suit), Galatians (Berlin Wall), The Times

vi. ESD ISM AU 6G **(as Knowledge)**
Herald Heaven->1st Resurrection to Renaissance Route (Terrain, Rocket Throw Back Next Isle, Supernova, Deuteronomy) – Theta (Ezra/Nehemiah)
Graded Axis X (Business Suit), Judea (Great China Wall), Street Times

v. IR GSM KRE 3G **(as Secular)**
Hologram Pentecost->**DNA Rhythm Body Blockage**
Utopia->Third World Route (Mountain, Train Express *Next Clan, Serbia Dust, Leviticus) – Sigma (Jobs/Proverbs)
Small Loop (African Suit), Titus (Sambal Wall i.e. 38), New York Times

vi. RF **NR** DPRK 5G **(as Dream)**
Holy See->**Mindset Brain Harmonic Blockage**
Renaissance->First World Route (Isle, Ship Departure *Next Adventist, Pearl, Noel) – Lambda (Passover, Easter, Christmas, Halloween)
Big Loop (Christmas Suit), Philemon (Israel Wall), Herald Times

Y625. Christian Mathematics XXX: The Sambals Technology those Military Technology Breakthrough required Final Bridging means Rainbow (Whitepaper)

i. **Blueprint Economy – Biomedical Technology** ('prior of Infrastructure Economy)

a.k.a. Genealogy Biblical Genetic Cryptography Calligraphy Climate linked to Earth Science Economy

ii. **Rare Earth Economy – Metallurgy Technology**

a.k.a. Scalar Machine e.g. Welding ('prior of Clean Energy Economy)

Privacy Issue
The Civil Law the International Sea Meta Law
Immigration and Air Traffic Genocide

Based on
Citizen Age & Carrier Weighted
Immigration Law implementation

Issue on
Anti Semitic & Anti True Love

Scalar Machine e.g. Welding

iii. Knowledge Economy – Nanotechnology ('prior of Digital Economy)

a.k.a. Metrology

Y653. War Insight XXXXII: Revealed of Shanghai 1943 due to Dispute Chinese Democracy the University and Chinese Royal the Church (Whiteboard)

Chinese Dispute on Christianity started on Shanghai in 1923' and 1823', and 2023'.

There are majority only 1 sect of Christian within Global that time. The Protestant and the Catholic was merge with All with Protestant become the Fundamentalist Methodist Globally.

The Famous 1st Charismatic Wave spread from United States to Singapore since 1823' the California Washington to Singapore Raffles the Aboriginal Chinese the Pioneer until today become into the Anak Pelangan the Abraham Offspring of Chinese a.k.a. Moon River Dust.

This stirred up the extinction of Malaysia Singapore Chinese threat in 1923'. The battle was with Taiwan Union the Democrat Army of Sun Yat Sen' Repel Army. This Repel Army yield due to Conspiracy against the Hitler led Nazi Massacre of Gas Poison toward Germany Citizen mostly the Poland Jew and Germany Jew i.e. Cell Schism of Church the Charismatic.

The side story was arisen with Malaysia Aboriginal of Penang the Democracy Oversea University Graduated the Chinese Mafia as well as Malaysia Royal Inclined Traitor. Hence, this makes Chinese Refugee started inflows from China, Hongkong, Malaysia to Singapore started in 2023'.

Hence, the Church Reformation was in Singapore the Chinese Nativity and Book of Life the 100 years squeezed the fifth times since Buckingham the 1st called British Reformation of Anglican formed and 2nd the Japan Imperial Army the Democracy formed before 1800s'.

And so on the Hongkong Macao failed on this trend due to the Colony of Japan Mafia the Spread Sheet of Chinese Mafia into Drug Reseller the Mass and Chaos.
Goes on this, the Wall Treasure of Christianity revealed in 1938' the hidden conspiracy celebration events tragedy in Japan.

The Treasure of this has tension on Germany Security Bank in Europe to United Kingdom Commonwealth Congress on Asia. The Wall & War of Series started in these Outcoming yield many weapons of undesirable into threat of Medicine discovery of Dead End.

Into of this, the American Jew begin the exodus into Space a series until today. And the Christian Treasure is indeed the Islam Treasure and

Buddhism Treasure Residue Products majority the Biblical Genealogy Medicine.

Other than Treasure, the Charismatic Wave spread bring along the Democrat Army of Sky Lock the Sky Weapon of Computer Lock and Body Inner Ear Lock.

The Military Technology Advantage of Western continues led the Decryption of Treasure into Heaven Making the Economy Harvest the fully. i.e. Promised Land of Chinese. Unsurprised, Chinese turns this down into full use of Christian Bible into Technology Development of Space Economy than Developed their weapon into Christian Wall & War.

The outcome become Security Chinese of Refugee and Chinese Marriage Misconducting Defect of Many fields, the Modern Civilisation Era. The Peace conspiracy of Chinese due to Hatred of Shanghai Army and Scholar. And this is the famous Shanghai 1943' Legend and Singapore Malaysia 1963' Legend, Taiwan Hongkong Macao Merge 2000' Legend.

The going forward, the Pearl Harbour Schism of God Kingdom Advent and 911 New York Tower Schism of God Kingdom Advent bring terrorism of Nuclear Weapon and Air Disaster into series of Conspiracy against Church Reformation. The present property as majority from the Fruitsful outcome of rip and sow of Christian and Treasure of Heaven into Full Countermeasure against Genocide when Christian goes Matured and graduated.

This is the reminder of Tradegy and Fruits Harvest at the same time. And Charismatic Success and Catholic Orthodox Success at the same time too. Church has becoming Unity if only the Technology development has reached Maturity. Thence is the best church and many to come to Chinese reaching, when World War has brings dead alive the 2nd in 2023' either.

Yes, Charismatic is the Culprit among.

Errata 21Mar2023

Volume 4: Man Made Cored

For Sigma Only

折回者

Y601. Criminology XXX: Economic Belt & 16per Dust the Individual Crime Tendency *(Census)*

Israel Nativity of 6 Chronicle Era
Olive Economic Belt the 6 kinds.
Organic Lambda Index same, #9. The quantum dust. i.e. Salted Fibre

Manna Origin: ISR (2nd), Gross Capital Federation
Kiwi Origin: AU (3rd), Gross Capital Federal
Peanut Origin: UK (4th), Biblical per Capita
Olive Origin: RUS (5th), Biblical per Capita
Pineapple Origin: MY (6th), Meta per Capita
Mint: SG (1st), Meta per Capita

Economic Belt defined as Trade Deficit Belt Ranked. Lock Trade Zone and Free Trade Zone.

e.g. India. Prime Rank is Singapore due to Strait Dust of High Rank the Moon River Dust of #16. It will ultimately become Organic, from Dust to Organic, the Original Image of God.

Hence, the International Meta Law can made. Naval Sea Law thence. As long as China was Lock down as *Renaissance Dynasty throw back the Lock Trade Zone.*

Spider net: Hierarchy search engine method

Example:

Dust #1: Fibre Net
Dust #16 Strait, the famous Moon River Dust
Dust #9 Quantum Dust, the Olive New Israel. i.e. Parallel Eden Garden Footage Milestone.

Y602. Biblical Application: Bible Translation Version Selection Guides (Broadcast)

Yellow Collar Crime: 3x Blacklist (Criminal, Motive), Conspiracy Thinktank
White Collar Crime: 3x Whitelist (Misconduction, Colony), Guinea Scapegoat

I. Intellect Holy Spirit: CCB
– Vatican i.e. Schism (Galatians)
Eschatology Holy Spirit: NIV
– Pentecostal i.e. Apostolic (Corinthians)
Eucharist i.e. Fellowship, ASV Translation
- Puritan i.e. Extra (Philippian)

I. Biblical Holy Spirit: CUV
– Lutheran i.e. Biblical (Ephesian)
Etymology Holy Spirit: NKJV
– Herald Charismatic i.e. Alternative (Philemon)
Yield of Canon i.e. Christology, Tyndale Translation
– Catholic i.e. Old to New Hebrew (Colossian)

III. Generic Holy Spirit: CSB
– Christmas Nativity i.e. Tither Account (Hebrew)
Redemption Holy Spirit: KJV
– Fundamentalist i.e. Theology (Jude)
Holy See i.e. Circle of Fifth, ESV Translation
– Episcopal i.e. Reformed (Titus)

Y620. Biblical Application: Selection of Gospel the Synaptic (Broadcast)

i. Luke Gospel
Oriental Fig Tree has reached Mile End
Agency the Exchange
UN Democrat Socialist
Alternate Hero: **Apostolic Church**
As Genius/Paralysis: Devil/Mary

ii. Matthew Gospel
Olive when Peanut liked Manna
Holding the Trade
NATO Nationalist Socialist
Extra Hero: **Agency University**
As King/Beggar: False Christ/Nazareth & Messi 1st

iii. Mark Gospel
Fig Tree the Rose
Foundation the Vault
WWF Communist Socialist
Alternate Villain: Satan/Chris

iv. John Gospel
Oriental Olive the Dust Peanut
Congress the Treasure
KMT Nationalist Democracy
Graded Civilian: **Chancellor Bank**
As Magician/Crazy: Serpent/Stevenburg

v. Luke Gospel
Oriental Fig Tree the Silicon Rose
Agency the Exchange
NASA Democracy Socialist
Extra Villain: Man of Sins/Jesuit

vi. Mark Gospel
Fig Tree eventually has Leaf
Foundation the Vault
WHO Monarchy Democrat
Graded Hero: **Remote Laboratory**
As President/Criminal: False Prophet/Elizabeth

6 Dust-liked Meta
A. New York Timezone, +5min, +1 (Conspiracy Route)
B. Shanghai Timezone, +30min, +6 (Earthquake Route)

C. Geneva Timezone, -30min, -6 (Tsunami Route)
D. Moon River, +25min, +5 (Pandemic Route)

E. Fig Tree Timezone, -25min, -5 (Terrorism Route)
F. London Timezone, -5min, -1 (Crime Route)
Errata 26Mar2023

Y623. Biblical Application: Commuting of Love the Marriage, Commuter of Love the Family (Broadcast)

i. I Generations: Exodus Omega 90s' Sheppard Dog
II Generations: **Expatriate Cell Schism, Desperado**, Y2k' Sigma
(Elders & Juniors, Sow & Rip Value i.e. Royalty), Grace Affiliated/Exposure e.g. Kitkat
Doer, Fig Tree the Franchised
Developed/Global Class Country, Western Continental
Gland Sky Continental, Blue Sky Continental
US/AU Israelite Polish British 粤 South Sea China 南海, 上海

ii. Alpha Rolls: Royalist 50s' Dragon
Omega Rolls: **Traveller Royalist Traitor, Presidential,** 60s' Lambda
(**Father Dating Number i.e. Loyalty**), **Reflection Fwd/Bwd e.g. Sony Stakeholder, Olive i.e. Manna the Original**
Developing/Multinational Country, Asia Peninsular.
Coral Strait, Pearl River
MY/TW Hebrew Gothic Canaan 杭 Resin River China 江南, 珠江

iii. RY Series: Babybooms 70s' Unicorn
RQ Series: **Refugee Regime Repel, Apostolic**, 80s' Epsilon
(**Mother Carrier Weighted i.e. Lent**), **Generic AtoZ e.g. Texas Thinker, Oriental Olive i.e. Pineapple the Branded**
Third/First World i.e. Universal, South East Asia Isles.
Coral Isle, Guinea Isle
SG/IND Jewish Jude Judea 津 Mt East China 山东, 北越

*The Meta Image' Reflection of these is
Blooded Dating Father,
Blooded Carrier Mother,
Blooded Beared Elders & Juniors

Y632. Christian Finance Z2: The Quantum unity Harvest Theory - Currency Theorem (Review)

Debt of Currency is TT the arbitrary account of evil. Retailer. Where the Buyer is not beneficial either. The currency of Federal stil the most choice. and the rootcause of pass conspiracy the initiaves agasint Russian Federation UN.

The resolution has one in mindset in which grossing of all currency into digital bank. hence make trade zone of exchange as well as deficit exchange of gross.

The venue is Queen issue Currency Security Bank in Australia the Jewish forever land.

The Chinese Security threat are from Australia covering. The Academy University of Royalism to Chinese. among US,UK

The vulnerability of Federation RUS once again rebuke us the Chinese Security as whole burden suit of Democracy into Chinese than African.

Simply '64' event the crabs. or 911 the Crabmachine thence. This is a teaching that Tension of Church is among the biggest issue of all history and future.

The dispel of gentile is irritating false lawsuit of growing by this kind of attitude of Satan Devil bunches.

We chinese required the Unity of Meta in against the False Meta split toward us, primely,. and this is automatic and naturally unless Anti Semitic arose or
anti true love arose.

Hence, to breakthough into Economic Harvest and Advent God Kingdom of Happiness we ought to stay in gross. nor even schism can harms.

Polarised is always 7right and correct. The white lie. and white light. of passiveness.

1% of voltage into temperature. The Quartz liked. In view as now, the Financial product has no yield at all due to singularity.

Malaysia has the unique advantaged due to our currency tend to against the gross. called maverick currency the token cents.

This is imagine as bitcoin cryptography coin as inititiative of collect duty free lamer.

Vault or Crab House is the most populated.

Boxing., Tiger Show, Comic. Hollywood Blaster not the opposed Suit.

Soccer, Masaki, Library Tea House, or Netflix the Korea Drama.

but UK okay. Currency differnce has the says. Pound is purity in weighted. Token is shielded in least hall mark. Called Service Tax or Tips. the Government Tithered.

Culture of man and women makes this. And rule out the Mafia HQ and hostage inaugural hideout.

Y635. Social Engineering XXVIII: 属土，属尘，属天的仿制品科技之升华版 (Forum)

i. Adventist - Moon (Sand Isle, Modern, Airport), Spiritual Entity – Unicorn (Easter), Nazareth Meta Merge->Web Teleport (Router Mesh, Homeplug, Skynet Nerve Control)
vs Lion Body Human Face, Linger against Ancient (Terrestial Land Federal, Office, Ashed (Book of Esther, Burg->Berg/Meta Merge, *Grace of Spiritual Body)/Semitic Skin, King Made, 3per #7 Timezone Clan), Organic into Gel (**Natural Death, UV->ESD Motorised Weapon**), Solution: *Tinted Wired Glass Window (Apollo Rocket, against Ship Vegan)*
Abraham: IR DNA Cluster the Residue->Chromosome Navigation->Traveller Aboriginal (Queen Made)
White Dragon (Hardcore)
NGO vs Consultacy Office (African Chicken liked, 99:1, Meta Merge of 7 Sealed Meta Fade into 1 Sealed)(Prophet Malachi, Puppet, Omega), Revelation
Kulai Berlin Wall, Resort Road vs Stulang Schism Road, Hill Road
Gothic vs Hebrew (Fire Lake, US/HK/JB/DPRK/AFR)
Corinthians (Dust) vs Hebrew
Filled with Evil Spirit Motive->Christian Cult (Vital)

ii. Oriental - Mars (Coral Isle, Metropolis, Harbour), Spiritual Body – Dragon (Halloween), Quantum Sky Merge->Hologram Bruteforce (Router Gun, High Voltage Lens)
vs Trojan Horse, Zombie against Future (Valley Land Federation, Polish (Book of Nehemiah, Claus->Clause/Too Many, *Grace of Holy Spirit)/Japanese Skin Clay God Made, 12per #14 Timezone Clan), Dust into Organic (**Sudden Death, Fatal Disease & Tumour**), Solution: *Magnetic Ferrite Shield*
Dark Dragon (Escort)
Adam: EMF RNA Conceived->Genetic Staging->Refugee Diaspora (King Made)
Uniforms vs Clinical Laboratory (Japanese Duck liked, 50:50, Meta Fade into 1 Sealed)(Prophet Zechariah, Sheppard Dog, Alpha->Original), Old Testament
Pontian Milestone Road, Canyon Road vs Skudai Olive Road, Silk Road
Jude vs Jewish (First World, RUS/MY/KL/JPN/THAI)
Titus (Gel of Adam or Serpent a.k.a. Rib *Calcium Dating Number i.e. Hymn Rating, Complex Salted Light i.e. Isle Mapping) vs Judea
Fallen down to Gentile Soul Motive->Satan Cult (Viral)

*27 time zone Eden Garden Milestonte at same coring configuration Organic & Dust & Gel, 6 lock 6666 chronicle era, parallel' junction at New Year Eve

31st lock 6every year Solar calendar met with Lunar calendar yield Comet Calendar lock10 metric

iii. Promised Land - Sky High (Spacious Isle, Clan, Railway), Spiritual Material – Sheppard Dog (Passover), Jesuit Pentecost Merge->Netbus Porting (Router Magnet, UPS, Heart beat Intelligence)
vs Lost & Found, Cranberries against Modern (Grass Land Governor Tower, Urban, Terrace, Inked (Book of Ezra, Sky->Ski/Lift off Skew, *Grace of Soul)/Germans Skin, 9per #16 Timezone Clan), Gel into Dust (**Vegetable Death, Chemistry Weapon**), Solution: *Ioniser Gas Compressor (Oriental Express Train, against Rocket Residue)*
Noel: UV mmDNA Organised->Viral Jumping->Expatriate Indigeneus (Man Made)
Black Dragon (Freelance)
Yellow Collar vs Multinational Governor Tower (Germans Pig liked, 40:60, Meta Split into 7 Sealed, Meta Merge of 7 Sealed)(Prophet Habakkuk, Pekinese, RY), Gospel
Perling Fig Tree Road, Wall Road vs Masai Mile End Road, Airport Road
Polish vs Israelite (Hell, AU/TW/PN/KRE/IND)
Philemon (Organic) vs Colossians
Monster Body Motive->Anti God Mafia Crime Syndicate (Virus)

Ultimate Escape:
Catechism (Book of Life): Doctrine Judification Carrier vs Etymology Carrier
Wife i.e. Dust Value Prospect – Prison Social (Rip)
Father i.e. Stone Value Net Worth – Childhood Social (Dating)
Brother i.e. Diamond Value Net Worth – Retired Social (Patch)
Sister, Dramatic, Horoscopic Meta (Sow)
Mother i.e. Dust Value Prospect – Heaven Social (Carrier)
Holy Spirit Milestone: Better Journey

The first man was of the dust of the earth; the second man is of heaven. 1 Corinthians 15:47
第一个人是出于地，是属尘土的；第二个人是出于天。哥林多前书 15:47

爱是一生一世，信是永生永世，望是今生今世. 此话一出，万水难滩，覆水难收，而路有过之不及也.

Errata 18Mar2023

Y664. Criminology XXXIII: Working from Home Platform, Gentile Sky Platform, and Meta Disorder Platform at Eucharistic Final Day (Census)

i. **Time Lock**, Gym less Body – Genetic Chronography Disorder ZION
Soul of God vs Gentile vs Ghost
timezone & communication protocol mindsets – crazy or in love loyalty
Meta Spirit Soul behavior – **Hell Route Trojan Horse** (27per Generation **Meta Carrier Split Easter to Halloween to Habakkuk Day**)(Land Grace 麻油地, 6 Knots Mile End Job Conference)(Time Metric Fade (Anti Genocide), Chained Train vs Royal Boat on Orthogonal) **on the track/endervour** Lock27 Christmas Day (Lower End Loop), to Harvested the Heavenly Town)

ii. **Sky Lock**, Wireless home – Wicked Calligraphy Identity FBI
Angelic vs Linger (Coring) vs Villain
quantum weapon remote control behavior – mania or consecutive tasked agape
Quantum Holy Spirit language command – **Fire Lake Route Word Prison** (10per Series **Warrant Carrier Mapping, Holy Night to Christmas to Boxing Day**)(Sky Grace 天公, 9 into 1 Ruth Demography)(Sky Merged (Anti Climate Change), Ship AtoZ vs Bus AtoJ, Lock 9 New Year Eve (All demography), Homogenous) **departure/resurrected** to Modern Current Era)

iii. **Footage Lock**, Working at home – Distrusted Cryptography Credential CIA
Creature vs Alienic vs Zombie
frauded keylock language command – stupid or head damage romance
Pentecost mindsets – **First World Route, Colony** (12per Rolls **Solace Carrier Fade, Passover to Lent to Pentecostal Day**)(Sea Grace 大海, each 1 take Chronicle Metrology)(Sea Isled (Anti Nuclear Weapon), Graded Rocket vs Concept Car, Holistic, Lock12 Pentecost Day (CP Rating Class) **Fallen/Risen** to New Isle Config' Map)

Errata 30Mar2023

Y665. Criminology XXXIV: Correlation of Law, Synaptic of Law, hence the Skew of Law (Census)

Moses Law vs Sarah Law vs Angelo Law

Social Law vs Economic Law vs Ergonomic Law

Skew of Law vs Synaptic of Law (Discreet) vs Correlation of Law (Conjugated)

Lawmaker vs Apostolic vs Sainthood

Islam *Extreamist vs Herald Discreet vs Buddhism Conjugated*

2per Dark Dragon vs 2per White Dragon vs 2per Black Dragon
A to Z, a to z

*Innocent Criminal vs Momentum Sinner vs Desperado Becker->***Flying Dragon (Ancient Dragon)(Federation UN), Mafia Army, Socialist the Democrat***
Hierarchy University is not Democracy.
Salted Light
Oriental Democracy

*Weapon Criminal vs Repeater Sinner vs Desperado Housewife->***Sheppard Dog (Ancient Dragon)(Multinational UN), Nazi Army, Republican the Royalist***
Flatted University is Democracy.
Combustion Residue
African Democracy

Y677. End World Backup Plan the Final Resort Approach (Census)

99:1 12perc immediately, Crab Cored
99:1 9per depend on Adventist, Windows Cored
40:60 6per long term stability 5G mDNA extra cored, Apple Cored
Charismatic Wave Fasci UN Multinational
poise threat on series Conspiracy Crime.
Resolution: has to Unity 99:1,
Versus 1 vs 1
40:60 Islam Ally vs Buddhism Ally
*10 years Lock 10, is time squeeze of whole Chronicle 5000 years Unit of Full Sambal River Journey & Rainbow 6 Bridge, the New Jerusalem i.e. Eden Garden Footage, Revolutionary and Heavenly Formed.
Time squeeze feasible only if A-Z suit Generic Top 25 % percentile meet Qualification Standard, Populated Standard, to make reality.

i. Church Reformation when if Adventist Conditions meets. Kelvin Mark Conjugated onto Universe Con-formatting, hence after Climate Change. And, Fahrenheit Hue Harmony onto Geothermal Escalating, hence before Global Warming.
After Cold War interpose with World War "Mexico/Israel Wall/Berlin Treasure"
Adventist to Oriental (Express Train, Speed Boat) to Final Resort
Western Nativity AU MY Christ Town 5G cored <->10G i.e. 2.4G cored
George Town RUS UK US **Final Generations** A.D. 2033'
Stellarhood Scene – Union & Church Chronicle Era
Christ Habour, A-Z Same Heritage Platform, Flea Market Spiritual Terrace
Blueprint Cast Out Footprint – 10G Rare Earth Economy (Anti True Love Burden)

ii. Chinese Speed Evangelism, the Famous "Chinese Mass", i.e. Democracy Politic Revolution stir up the "Chinese Royalism the Guinea Colony Dispute" against with Semitic, Western, Far East, India and Manchu as well as Islam Jihad.
Civil War/Terrorism War "Great Chinese/Korea Sambas Wall Treasure"
Promised Land – Chinese Ethnic Re-shuffle Main land Isle and All Christ Town Isle. (Tesla Car) to 10per Unlock the Demography Fellowship
Chinese Nativity SG TW HK Funky Town **Next Generations** A.D. 2028'
Joker Scene – New Standard Technology Era
J-suit, A-J Same Weather Platform, Fighting Unlock to Hell Unlock
Blueprint Layered On Footwell – 8G Blueprint Economy (Anti Natalie Christian Burden)

iii. Church Evolution if Medicine Renaissance Framework the Biomedical the "Holistic Medicine i.e. Gross Deficit Science cum Spiritual a.k.a. Christian Medicine Salted Light, Cost Free Mileage" vs "Royal Mental Medicine Self Lighten, Cost End Mileage" vs "Pseudo Clinical Medicine Light Powered, High Cost Mileage", overtaking desirable e.g. Humanity Crime, the Variety of Singularity Crime so called Veterinary Related Crime.

Racial Riot/Currency War "Silk Road Wall/Strait Wall Treasure"
Renaissance – Copycat Suspected Gospel Leak (Rocket or Ship to Present Isle Mapping if Demography has high Lent with No Gross Subsidy)(Commuting instead of Commuter)(Upgrade)
Utopia – Copycat Suspected Gospel Leak (Rocket or Ship to Present Isle Mapping if Demography has high Lent with No Gross Subsidy)(Commuting instead of Commuter)(Upgrade)
Islam Nativity MY BRU INDIA ARAB **1st Generations** A.D. 2023'
Ancient Dragon Scene – Dynasty the Contemporary Era
Messi & Ruth, Series Mapping, Church Legislation redefine
Blueprint Projection Footage – 6G Knowledge Economy, 7G Uniform Duty Economy (Anti Semitic Social Bonding Burden)

Y678. End World Backup Plan the After Life Capital (Bulletin)

i. Graded Cored vs Fire Lake Route – Adventist
Gels liked, Glass, Carbon – **Quarantine->Meta Cropped Word Prison** (Nerve Disease)(Isle Lent, Eschatology Calendar Lent, Ezra)
(University for Chinese, Democracy->Democrat Apostolic)**(Tax Collection or Accompanied, Olive Road to Schism Road)**
(Timezone disorder, Isle Mapping Fixed Reynold Duty), UV (Jacob)
Free R-suit Wisery, Reynold Duty & Global Class State **(Perpetual Energy)**

ii. Extra Cored vs Hell Route – Oriental
Dust liked, Rib, Fibre – **Clinical->Guinea Colony** (Chronic Disease)(Terrace Royalty, Ecumenical Judification Royalty, Ether)
(Semitic Reconciliation, Republican->Federation Military)**(Judges Remastered or Anthropology, Silk Road to Great Chinese Wall)**
(Calendar Discreet, Terrace Rolling Fixed Psi Duty), EMF (Adam), IR (Noel)
Free C-suit Rohs, Psi Duty & Multinational Clans **(Growth of Puritan)**

iii. Alternate Cored vs 1st Resurrection Route vs 2nd Resurrection Route – Promised Land
Clay liked, Bone, Organic – **Prison->Intelligence Ransom (Acute Disease)**(Community Loyalty, Etymology Affiliated Naming Loyalty, Nehemiah)
(Religion Diplomacy, Communist->Socialist Technology)**(Accommodated to Publicised, From Fig Tree to Canyon Road)**
(Kelvin Mark Rating, Community Generation Fixed Celsius Duty), ESD (Abraham)
Free J-suit Apollo, Celsius Duty & Hierarchy Demography Clans **(Abundance of Food)**

Y682. Raise the New Marketplace Land against the Social Re-engineering toward Chinese (Forum)

Malaysia has no edge on Social Bonding the Imperialism. Social Biased to African Democracy instead of Chinese Democracy. The Technology Emperor in most Asia has met this obstacle to overcome.

Hence, Malaysia becoming the hot point of Crime conspiracy, and highest trained Samuel Technologist. And Singapore chosen the Strait Wall to prevent this kind of hopping into their land.

But it has meet difficulty due to Church Cell Schism Army Anti Semitic dominant Singapore. The Repel Army hence yield the new comer Air Fighter Pilot and Dog Fight Motorist.

However, this has come to the remarks, when the Computer World has new brainstorm on Replica Weapon of Cheap price. This replica Weapon is main weapon of Korea Army and so called Hebrew Army in Singapore. The Cell Schism of Israel Empire the Global Class.

Without the Social Bonding and Montage of Duty Free, these Area would be No Living Activities. But with Duty Free montage or Social Bonding to boost the Samuel Technology Empire.

The Necking of Global Class could on track become the New Jerusalem, the New Market Place of Commercial the Free Trade Immigration Land all the years. Hence, the IT ecommerce would has home now, at condition of Free Time Waived.

Volume 5: New +-X/ Standard

For Techno Fever Only

科技发烧友

Example Application:

5.1. Azure – *Computer Rejuvenate Climate*

Y797. Time Zone Era Evolution (Whitepaper)

Y780. Hybrid Engineering Part 12: IBM Azure TPM & Crabmachine, Apple & Watson & Guardian (Review)

Y771. Chronicle to Heaven Application (Whiteboard)

Y752. Telecommunication & Book of Life Insight (Census)

Y747. Crabmachine Design Guide (Trade Secret)

5.2. Watson – *Computer Rejuvenate Genealogy*

Y807. Computer Security Errata for Privacy & Safety As whole (Bulletin)

Y772. Property Etymology (Whitepaper)

5.3. Crabmachine – *Computer Rejuvenate Universe*

Y796. Authentication, Chronography, Metrology & Navigation Insight (Whitepaper)

Y750. Space Technology the Universe Insight (Whitepaper)

5.4. Guardian – *Computer Rejuvenate Medicine*

Y782. Architectural Material Replacement as Traditional Medicine, the Authentic Etymology Medicine Treatment (Journal)

Y776. Etymology Medicine (Journal)

5.5. Davinci – *Computer Rejuvenate Engine*

Y814. Hip Hop Box Design Guidelines (Whitepaper)

Y785. Man & Women Meta & Logistic Machine (Whitepaper)

Y784. Commuting Know how (Forum)

Y761. Economic Resolution Model e.g. Very High Gini Index amid Biblical Villain (Review)

5.6. Rohs – *Computer Rejuvenate Housing*

Y813. Politic Evolution Programs (Census)

Y805. 4 Type of Housing (Forum)

Y803. Fraud Material Identification & Industrial Revolution the Correlation 3 times (Whitepaper)

Y800. Building Material Protocol Rohs (Whitepaper)

Y799. Building Control System (Whitepaper)

Y798. Two Essential of Human Kind & Currency Ransom (Post)

5.1. Azure – Computer Rejuvenate Climate

Y771. Chronicle to Heaven Application (Whiteboard)

A. 3 Invention - Computer, Machine, Enclosure 防火，防水，防风，防雷 (God Misconduction, Climate War a.k.a. Sky War)
Croyalflush Quantum Computer Skeleton of Time – Anti Climate Disaster
Lite Car Hybrid with Reynold Light Milling – Anti Terrorism Commuting Barrier
Crabmachine Pilgrim Enclosure – Anti Medicine Bottleneck of Hygiene

B. 4 Economics Model from Car Engine Development (Man Misconduction, Terrorism War)
防虚，防暗，防金 i.e. Christian Persecution (Democrats Terrorism)
i. Common Celsius Zone i.e. Temperature Scale – Liberal Land, Freedom from Moses Law i.e. Promised Land – Free Flows
ii. Common Reynold Zone i.e. Flea Heritage – Easter Land, Freedom from Sarah Law i.e. Oriental – Free Licenses
iii. Common Psi Zone i.e. Puritan Time Metric – Christmas Land, Freedom from Covenant Law i.e. Adventist – Free Tuitions
iv. Common Tesla Zone i.e. Crypto Bottom Threshold – Virgin Land, Freedom from Marriage Law i.e. Utopia – Aged Lock

C. 3 Kings of Political Evolution 防光 (World War the New Age)
Timothy = Indian Semitic (Hindu Treasure = Bible Villain Definition, Pre-WWIII
Anti Genocide Imperial Blueprint
Thesssalonians = Chinese Semitic (Christian Treasure = Holy Spirit Definition), WWII
Anti Industrial Mass Destruction Weapon Duty Blueprint
Philemon = Malay Semitic (Islam Treasure = Semitic Definition), WWI
Anti Economic Poverty GDP Demography Blueprint

D. 2 people 防实，防虚 i.e. Semitic Persecution (Royalism Terrorism)
Buckingham Palace – Royalism, Semitic Security Bank – Chronicle Whitelist
White House Royalism – Royalism, Chinese Security Bank – Eschatology Whitelist
Blue house Democrats – Democrats, Indian Security Bank – Etymology Whitelist
Vatican Democrats – Democrats, Jewish Security Bank – Ecumenical Whitelist

Y797. Time Zone Era Evolution (Whitepaper)

Time Era Evolution
@Earth Geology
@Medicine Man Kind
@Ecosystem

To find out how the Time Zone Mileage can varies according to Carbon Dating. The Skeleton Calendar play a critical part.

And the Man Kind Genealogy can only perform more than 4per Time Zone is a great prominent discovery of abundancy in terms of medicine automatic healings.
And hence the Earth geology as well as the Ecosystem of Sky Cloud follow the same accordance too.

The closure mapping of Time Zone originated from Jerusalem the Israel Time Zone arrangement as follow the New Nativity of Christian Reconciliation.

For that concerns, the Time Zone is replicating into Many phase in life not the least the academic but the various industrial such to dismissed the disruption of medicine system wage as secondary option.

Y780. Hybrid Engineering Part 12: IBM Azure TPM & Crabmachine, Apple & Watson & Guardian (Review)

A. Pancreas – Plotter – *AVR: Dogma a.k.a. Metrology Law incl. Hormone or Duty Deficiency (Nil) i.e. **Time Transducer ESD Compressor the UV Wifi a.k.a. Hubble Telescope** Footplot, *Hybrid/Roman *Material
Anti Nuclear
Cleanser: Antique & Drug 物

B. Lung – Fuel Cell – UPS i.e. Transformer/Inverter: Sarah Law a.k.a. Tax Law incl. Organised Duty Free as the Tither Duty (Captain) i.e. **TPM Security Box ESD Transmitter/Receiver IR Wifi a.k.a. James Webbs Telescope** Footprint, *Greek *Medicine
Anti Pandemic
Material: Architecture
Medicine & Material 人

C. Sex Gland – Modem – Online UPS: Antenna the EMF Wifi a.k.a. Galilee Telescope Footwell: Moses Law a.k.a. Economic Law incl. Mafia Human Right as Scribe Duty (Ego), i.e. Moses Code Arabic *Weather
Anti Tsunami
Broadcast:
Weather & Universe 天

D. Heart – Regulator – Interactive AVR: Mesh **RF Bluetooth** Footage: Music Covenant a.k.a. Logistic Law incl. Cult Privacy as Pharisee Duty (Idol), i.e. Circle of Fifth, Latin *Spiritual
Anti Terrorism
Intelligence
Pentecost & Vegetable 地

5.2. Watson – Computer Rejuvenate

Genealogy

Y747. Crabmachine Design Guide (Trade Secret)

Transformer 8G/3G IBM 3-in-1 Geothermal UN Family/Social Polarity Spiritual Holistic

Crabmachine 5G/10G Android 1-in-4 Economics NATO Crime/Ecosystem Nativity Demography Individual

Ironman 10G/5G HP 4-in-1 Climate NASA Health/Charisma Footage Mapping Homogenous

UFO 3G/8G Macintosh 1-in-3 Carrier ZION Disaster/Harbour National Duty Union

Vatican Financial Rating i.e. Christian Wall a.k.a. Peter Castle Terrorism Dilation 祥 热

e.g. IELTS Geometric

Meta Principle i.e. Biblical Genetic a.k.a. Eden Garden Economics Solution 禄 电

e.g. DNA Crypto

Moses Law Recalculation i.e. Culture Legislation a.k.a. New Jerusalem Puritan Marriage 福 光

e.g. Codec Parametric

Commercial Law i.e. Sarah Law a.k.a. Christ Harbour Anti Pandemic 寿 风

e.g. Rohs Capital

Y752. Telecommunication & Book of Life Insight (Census)

i. Oriental (Lover in/Family out, Sky, Emmanuel Cloud 以马内利云)
Etymology Naming or Watched Salvation
Streaming, Wifi, Internet, EMF TV, LTE 5G
Wifi Phone e.g. Zoom (High Lag, High Ping)
(for Celebrity Office 20per Meta a.k.a. Official Church) vs 3per Dragon Meta the Anti Christ (Dead End Mileage)

ii. Adventist (Union in/Lover out, Land, Obladi Oblada Cloud 方言圣徒云)
Catechism Justice or Gentile Salvation
Cable, Bluetooth, Intranet, RF Radio, GSM 3G
IP Phone e.g. Whatsapp (Short Lag, Low Ping)
(For Family 6per Meta a.k.a. First Family) vs 10000per Nazi Meta the Anti God (Long Journey Competing)

iii. Promised Land (Office in/Church out, Universe, Chronicle Cloud 编年史云)
Broadband, USB, World Wide Web
Eschatology Calendar or Chronicle Salvation
IR Facsimile, CDMDA 10G, Voice IP Phone e.g. Skype (Short Lag, Low Ping)
(For Lover 200per Meta a.k.a. First Lady) vs 1/7per Godness Meta the Anti Dogma (Dating Expired)

iv. Utopia (Family in/Union out, Sea, Pentecostal Cloud 五旬使徒云)
Ecumenical Baptism or Union Salvation
Dial Up, Lan, Ethernet
ESD Telephone, NR 8G, Analog Phone e.g. Telegram (Long Lag, High Ping)
(For Union 100per Meta a.k.a. Foundation) vs 10per Sigma Meta Anti Semitic (Biblical Villain)

Y772. Property Etymology (Whitepaper)

A. Face i.e. Inner Ear (Blood Pressure, Network) – **High Rise Cabinet i.e. Tither Rate a.k.a. Deaf or Blind**
Legs i.e. Skeleton (Time Learning Curve, Domain) – **Desktop Cabinet i.e. Dead End Mileage a.k.a. Brain Orifice Failure**
Hands to Arms i.e. Joints (Flash Memory) – **Hanger Cabinet i.e. Tither Developing a.k.a. Veterinary Flu**

B. Liver (Wisdom) – Printer, Piano, Guitar *Footprint Scale – **Sudden Tactile Failure or Feeling Failure a.k.a. Allergy Fever or Dogma Porting the Trojan Horse**
Lungs (Intelligence) – Studio Computer *Footage Clock – **Sudden Membrane Orifice Failure** or **Vocal Failure a.k.a. Popular Fever or Hearing Rooting the Paralysis**
Pancreas (Behavior) – Business Computer *Footwell Compression – **Sudden Motorised Failure or Emotional Disordered a.k.a. Common Fever or Veterinary Numb**
Kidney (Mental) – Toilet *Scar Fade Speed – **Chronic Disease or Chronic Guinea**
Sex Gland (Attitude) – Bath Tub **Friction Heat – Sudden Regulated Failure or Physiological Vision**

C. Bone (Connectivity Speed, Public Barrier) – **Meta Land Lord**, Mosaic, *Cable GSM/CDMDA – **Oncology or Acute Guinea**
Nerve (Shield Cored, Private Censored) – **Telecom**, *Wired NR **– Paralysis or Disabled**
Skins (Bandwidth, Fashion Crypto) – **Government**, *Wireless LTE – **Inflammation or Viral**
Gems (Family) – Library Cabinet **Purity Timeline – Nerve Disordered a.k.a. Epidermic *Fluid borne**
Ribs (Lover) – Locker Cabinet **Operation Gaps – Tooth Toxic a.k.a. Pandemic *Air borne**

Y807. Computer Security Errata for Privacy & Safety As whole (Bulletin)

A. Ant for VPN Firewall Software to Hardware – Humanity Crime, on Climate Disaster by Time Disorder Accident, Guinea by Identity Thief, Pandemic by Cookies Financial Sanction

B. Bug for Virtual Security Loophole Port, Passive Energy to Active Energy – Human right by Dogma Insurance Calendar Awareness e.g. Protestant as Anarchy, Porn as Peep, Dogma Backpack as Vet Drug

C. Spider for Footage Scanner, Max IP Dictionary as well as DNS Dictionary – Anti Dogma & Social by Brute Force, Twin Galaxy Personal Account Hiatus e.g. Internet Social Media

5.3. Crabmachine – Computer Rejuvenate Universe

Y750. Space Technology the Universe Insight (Whitepaper)

i. Oriental 3per- Lock 300years (Comet 彗星)
Wisery i.e. Ruth & Messi (Chronicle Samuel)
Trait: Hall Mark e.g. Sun Eclipse
3 Moon (Sky) – Share Same Ergonomics Calendar (e.g. Total 100 Surname Calendar 百家姓)
Union

ii. Adventist 10per – Lock 400 Years (South Polar 南极星)
Jesuit i.e. J-suit (Kings David)
Trait: Data Mark e.g. Bubble Crypto
18 Black Holes (Sea) – Share Same Time Metric (e.g. Total 9 Time Metric 九张脸)
Church

iii. Promised Land 2per – Lock 20Years (North Polar 北斗星)
Apollo i.e. Joshua (Jobs Ether)
Trait: Kelvin Mark Index Maturity, e.g. Bubble Tea
2 Sun (Universe) – Share Same Footage (e.g. Eden Garden 伊甸园)
Family

iv. Utopia 4per – Lock 1000 Years (Meteor 流星雨)
Maria i.e. Chris (Judges James)
Trait: Box Office e.g. Hollywood
6 Isometric of Earth (Mountain) – Share Same Vision (e.g. Satellite-liked Da Vinci Time Zone)
Lover

Y796. Authentication, Chronography, Metrology & Navigation Insight (Whitepaper)

Twin Galaxy@Iso Alternate, Oriental Western the Continental 4per (Pan Christian) vs Oriental Eastern the Great Eastern 4per (Pan Religion)->Iso Pentecost Code vs Iso Arabic Code

A. **Utopia 3G** GSM Iphone Scalar Commuting **KR** ->**Ether Garden i.e. Time Disorder Disaster Replicated i.e. Adam & Eve Dogma Illustration (For Christian Union Meta, Holy Wood) 7G** NR I Mac Mini Scalar Machine **SG** @Aircraft A-J Carbin – Constant kwh i.e. A-Z Market Zone Fire Wall **a.k.a. Dogma (No Crime Claimant)** @3phase, 0% Uniform Duty@High Meta Tax, Mileage Mixed Time Zone, CAP rating
Beidou the Maxwell #33 Satellite, New Christian Protocol (God Ministry conversion the Bridging Christian)

B. **Promised Land** a.k.a. Green Camp 5G Beidou **CN**->**Paradise i.e. High Cryptography Hierarchy Replicated e.g. Noel Ark, 9G** (For Islam Family Meta, Bollywood) AI Ipad Scalar Magic Pad ISR @Car Alpha Omega Seats – Low/High Sigma i.e. Universal Constant@Tyre the Global Natural Gas Populated, **a.k.a. Halal (No Disease Claimant)** kwh@3phase, CPPC rating 233volts@ref, Duty Free 80%:20% @High Income Tax, Mileage Free Time Zone
Authentic Christmas Nativity the Perfect Pilgrim Church e.g. Cathedral, Tabernacle etc. Reconciliation, North Polar #16 Moons as in Mar (Doctrinal Dogma Conversion of Pan Religion)

C. **Adventist** *a.k.a. Blue Camp **10G** LTE HP Watson **MY**->**Pure Land i.e. High Pilgrim Road Replicated e.g. Babel Tower (For Buddhism Office Meta, Buddha wood) 4G** IBM Azure CDMDA **JPN** Ortho Religion @Time Machine 1-10 Level – High/Low Sigma **a.k.a. Rohs (No Disaster Claimant)** @3phase, 33% Duty Overall@High Service Tax, Dead End Mileage, CP rating 239volts@ref
NASA I,II,III @Dust Disruption Comet a.k.a. Meteor Alpha Week, Beta Week, Omega Week (Theology Science Conversion of Pan Christian)

D. **Oriental 8G** (For LTE II Dell Crabmachine **HK**->Terminal to Three **Renaissance 6G** NR II Macintosh AWS **US** Ortho Christian @Space Ship A-Z Market Zone – 0kWh i.e. Halal @3phase, Entropy Equivalent Subsidiary, Free Duty@High Property Tax, High Mileage Time Zone, PC rating 241volts@ref

i. Terminal Renaissance the Ninth (Colourful Rainbow Liked Sky) via Adventist (XO Annealed Cloud) (For Union Baptist Authentic Christian) – **Major Church or Duty Schism** the Lutheran Leviticus equiv. Halal, South

Polar #18 Book of Revelation the 4 Creature @Aegean, Jupiter Train a.k.a. Reynold Renault Car 离子动力车 Boosted Horse Powered (*Tip: Car Windows), HK/MY, 8G@5G **Anti Crime Canonical Book of Corinthians** – Qualification: CPPC 33% Percentile, First World Duty Ransom Route 1% Percentile

ii. Terminal Adventist the Zee (Meta Horoscope Sky) via Promised Land (VSOP Tempered Cloud/Bubble Crusted Cloud) (For Pentecostal Calendar Watched Christian) – **Fundamentalist or New Christian Deuteronomy** the Covenant Forming equiv. Dogma Maxwell Solar #33 CPPC Rating the Final Populated Solar System @New Tyre Ship Psi Bandwidth Hyundai Car 宽带动力车 Assisted Robostness (*Tip: Car Radio), Tel' Avin SG/UK, 6G@2.4G **Anti Terrorism Canonical Book of Galatians** – Qualification: CP Rating 45% Percentile, Fire Lake Meta Dishonour Route 7% Percentile

iii. Terminal Promised Land the Omega (Colour Hue Sky) via Utopia (Milkly Pasteurised Cloud) (For Emmanuel Dogma Assurance Christian) – Innocent the Linger, Mass Exodus **a.k.a. Rohs, i.e. Linger**, Supernova #21 a.k.a. Blackjack @Renaissance, Pluto Celsius Proton Car 辐射动力车 Extended Mileage (*Tip: Car Radiator), TW/AU, 7G@6Eg **Anti Disease Canonical Book of Titus** – Qualification: CPPC rating 25% Percentile, Third World Famine Route 1% Percentile

5.4. Guardian – Computer Rejuvenate Medicine

Y776. Etymology Medicine (Journal)

1. Ribs (Lover) – Locker Cabinet Operation Gaps – Tooth Toxic a.k.a. Pandemic *Air borne (Moscow Timezone, Neck) -CIA

2. Face i.e. Inner Ear (Blood Pressure, Network) – High Rise Cabinet i.e. Tither Rate a.k.a. Deaf or Blind (Jerusalem Timezone) -Jerusalem

3. Legs i.e. Skeleton (Time Learning Curve, Domain) – Desktop Cabinet i.e. Dead End Mileage a.k.a. Brain Orifice Failure, Hands to Arms i.e. Joints (Flash Memory) – Hanger Cabinet i.e. Tither Developing a.k.a. Veterinary Flu (London Timezone, Feet) -UN

4. Liver (Wisdom) – Printer, Piano, Guitar *Footprint Scale – Sudden Tactile Failure or Feeling Failure a.k.a. Allergy Fever or Dogma Porting the Trojan Horse (China Timezone) -WWF

5. Lungs (Intelligence) – Studio Computer *Footage Clock – Sudden Membrane Orifice Failure or Vocal Failure a.k.a. Popular Fever or Hearing Rooting the Paralysis (Singapore Timezone, Hand tips) -WHO

6. Pancreas (Behavior) – Business Computer *Footwell Compression – Sudden Motorised Failure or Emotional Disordered a.k.a. Common Fever or Veterinary Numb (Japan Timezone) -World Bank

7. Kidney (Mental) – Toilet *Scar Fade Speed – Chronic Disease or Chronic Guinea (Geneva Timezone, Head) -NASA

8. Sex Gland (Attitude) – Bath Tub Friction Heat – Sudden Regulated Failure or Physiological Vision (Malaysia Timezone) -KMT

9. Bone (Connectivity Speed, Public Barrier) – Meta Land Lord, Mosaic, *Cable GSM/CDMDA – Oncology or Acute Guinea (Vatican Time, Stomach) – Vatican

10. Nerve (Shield Cored, Private Censored) – Telecom, *Wired NR – Paralysis or Disabled (Istanbul Timezone) -NATO

11. Skins (Bandwidth, Fashion Crypto) – Government, *Wireless LTE – Inflammation or Viral (Greece Timezone.Private) -ZION

12. Gems (Family) – Library Cabinet Purity Timeline – Nerve Disordered a.k.a. Epidermic *Fluid borne (New York Timezone) -FBI

Y782. Architectural Material Replacement as Traditional Medicine, the Authentic Etymology Medicine Treatment (Journal)

A. Ribs i.e. Heel & Toe (Lover) – Locker Cabinet Operation Gaps – *Wired NR 1G/NR II 6G/6.1G Carnival World Route, Pre-Bluetooth

same homogenous orthogonal vision – Paralysis or Disabled
Lizard & Cockroaches Plague 伤风 (UV Geothermal, the Upper Floor Radiation) vs Fabricated Calcium Fluoride ESD e.g. Drug Filled Cement Ashed Stone (Nicotine Bill)
Medicated Oil e.g. 斧标驱风油
Hygienic Mob combine with Inverter Commuting Machine e.g. Dyson (Reynold Cyclone)
Pancreas (Crypto Buffering): Ceramic Microstructure Antique e.g. 100 years Glass Bottle

WHO Medicine 医学 St. John: Products Thermal Microstructure Grain Boundary Scaled Degree (Ghost)

Home Class Decoration Products **a. Tempered (Foots) b. Annealed (Hands) c. Crusted (Head) d. Pasteurised (Stomach)**

B. Nerve Acne i.e. Basin Spinal (Shield Cored, Private Censored) – Telecom 3G/CDMDA 8G/3.1G Third World Route Post-Bluetooth

same footage orientated viewpoint, Nerve Disordered a.k.a. Epidermic *Fluid borne e.g. Avian
Cockroaches & Lizard Epidermic 寒疫 (RF Gravitational Frequency, the Underground Wave) vs Timbered Sulphuric Acid UV e.g. Maple Mosaic or Diamond Mosaic (Hormone Bill)
Medicated Oil e.g. 上标跌打油
Water Purifier combine with Inverter Commuting Machine e.g. Diamond (Psi Croast)
Sex Gland (Metric Archiving): Geology Diaphragm Membrane, Organism Living Culture e.g. A-Shampoo

NATO Architecture 建筑 Wisery: Spiritual (Angel)

Collection Class **Jewlery Antique** Products **a. Remote Creature b. Crusade Icon c. Metrological Chronographer d. Goddess Ego**

C. Gems Inflammation i.e. Bottom Artery (Family) – Library Cabinet Purity Timeline – *Wireless LTE/EVPO/LTE 3.5G Upside Down World Route, Pre-Wifi

same timeframe casting vision – Inflammation or Viral e.g. Mind Poison Cockroaches & Mosquito Pandemic 瘟疫 (IR Industrial Waste, the Abandon Chemical Heat Profile) vs Coated Metallic Sugar RF e.g. Sugar Coated Wax (Carbon Bill)
Medicated Oil e.g. 万金油
Refrigerator combine with Inverter Commuting Machine e.g. Yorks (Celsius Inverter)
Lung (Chrono Intelligence): Organic Radiation, Rare Earth Gravitational Cyclic Volcano Ashes e.g. Magnetic Crusted

NASA Space Science 太空 Apollo: Advanced Material (Linger)

Stage Class Jewlery **Decoration Products a. Gold Superconductor for Celsius b. Diamond Rock Harden for Lambda c. Silk Thickness Metric for Reynold d. Salt Powered for Psi**

D. Skins Corrupt i.e. Bottom Neck (Bandwidth, Fashion Crypto) – Government 5G/10G/2.4G First World Route Post-Wifi

same cryptography platform focus, Tooth Toxic a.k.a. Pandemic *Air borne e.g. AIDS
Rare Earth Gravitational Cyclic Volcano Ashes e.g. Magnetic Crusted
Rat Disease 鼠疫 (EMF Relativity Wind Speed, the Low Atmospheric Pressure) vs Ceramic Filled Rare Earth IR e.g. Mountain Hill Etching Glass (Viral Bill)
Medicated Oil e.g. 均隆驱风油
Air Purifier combine with Inverter Commuting Machine e.g. Daikin (Voltage Ioniser)
Heart (Meta Broadcast): Chemistry Catalyst Mechanism e.g. Natural Fruits Ranked

UN Technology 工艺 Galatians: Raw Material (Guinea)

Dairy Class **Pharmacy Products a. Fluoride for Metal (Water) b. Alcohol for timbered (Solar) c. Compound for resin (Air) d. Rubbered for fur (Dust)**

*Hygienic First Law= Momentum as Imperial Newton
*Hygienic Second Law=Burning as Imperial Gausian 1 to 1 only Turbulent.

Appendix
Utopia: F&B (Chinese), 10% Duty (Cult), Same Accompany

1. Tempered (Foots)
2. Remote Creature
3. Gold Superconductor for Celsius
4. Fluoride for Metal (Water)

Promised Land: MNC (Islam), 20% Duty (Labour), Same Venue

1. Annealed (Hands)
2. Crusade Icon
3. Diamond Rock Harden for Lambda
4. Alcohol for timbered (Solar)

Adventist: NGO (Semitic), 0% Duty (Cowboy), Same Timing

1. Crusted (Head)
2. Metrological Chronographer
3. Silk Thickness Metric for Reynold
4. Compound for resin (Air)

Oriental: SME (Japanese), 33% Duty (Professional), Same Casting

1. Pasteurised (Stomach)
2. Goddess Ego
3. Salt Powered for Psi
4. Rubbered for fur (Dust)

5.5. Davinci – Computer Rejuvenate Engine

Y761. Economic Resolution Model e.g. Very High Gini Index amid Biblical Villain (Review)

Requirement: Promotion on Anti Semitic Anti Dogma Anti God, Anti Christ or Economic Resolution the Greatest Recession Recovery

A. Oriental - 5D Cloud 五行 (Tempered Economic Model), Shared Calligraphy Zone
Journey required: Readiness Once off (Populated Census Calendar, Ship for Return), Egoism Mark a.k.a. Data Mark
Treasure Wall & War: Anthropology Terminal (God cored), Anti Automatic Weapon the Devil
Patriarch@Church: Sky War, Dog Fight World War (33% Percentile, Book of Life)

B. Adventist - 3D Cloud 三行 (Annealed Economic Model), Shared Crypto Zone
Journey required: 40 units (Oriental Express, Train for Family), Hall Mark the Box Office
Treasure Wall & War: Remastered to Puritan Route (Dogma), Anti Pandemic@False Prophet the Copycat Criminology Blueprint
Fatimah@Office: Star War, Fish Fight Cold War (12 Fruits of Tree)

C. Promised Land - 1D Cloud 单行 (Pasteurised Economic Model), Shared Metric Zone
Journey required: 30 units (Dragon Boat i.e. Car for Beyond), Hall Mark the Public
Treasure Wall & War: Commercial Time Metric Duty (Semitic), Anti Climate Change@False Christ the False Baptism
Rabbi@University: Sea War, Ant Fight Civil War (7th Seal of Heaven)

D. Utopia - 6D Cloud 意行 (Fresh Economic Model), Shared Geometric Zone
Journey required: 20 units (Fallen Satellite i.e. Rocket or Socialised), Kelvin Mark
Treasure Wall & War: Country Fruits the Hybrid DNA (King & Queen made), Anti Terrorism Guinea@ Ancient Dragon the Fraud Meta
Ruth@Family: Land War, Bird Fight Racial Riot (Jesus' Key of Hell)

Y784. Commuting Know how (Forum)

A. Oriental UN/KMT: Thermal Heat Economic Model by Mechanical Research
Holistic: Common Duty i.e. Common Federal Reserved
69 chain RNA Blueprint: Meta

B. Adventist NATO/CIA: War Crime Disruption Blueprint by Machine Recognition
Orthogonal: Common Union i.e. Moses Code a.k.a. Common Hall Mark
6.3 chain Chronicle Skeleton: Quantum

C. Promised Land NASA/FBI: Universe to Social Treasure by Metrological Chronography Archaeology
Aerial: Common GDP i.e. Common Voltage Threshold a.k.a. Common Commuting Populated
62 Etymology Surface: Pentecost

D. Utopia WHO/ZION: Pandemic Epidermic Norms Boundary by Semitic Congress
Homogenous: Mixed Crusted

Y785. Man & Women Meta & Logistic Machine (Whitepaper)

1-10 Graded Meta for Men for Ego (Train, Land)

A-Z Ranked Meta for men villain (Ship, Sea)

6 Chronicle Meta for Women from Gem (Rocket, Universe)

100 Meta for Women Ribs (Aircraft, Sky)

Y814. Hip Hop Box Design Guidelines (Whitepaper)

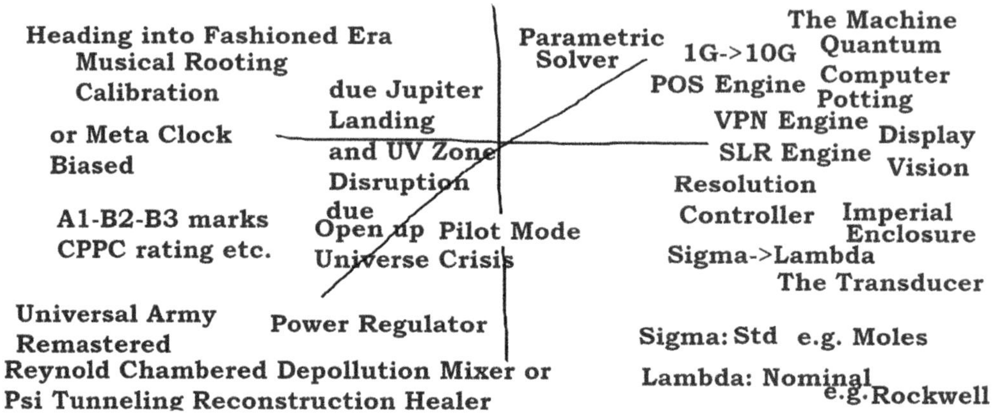
Heading into Fashioned Era
Musical Rooting
Calibration
or Meta Clock
Biased
A1-B2-B3 marks
CPPC rating etc.
Universal Army
Remastered
due Jupiter
Landing
and UV Zone
Disruption
due
Open up
Universe Crisis
Pilot Mode
Power Regulator
Reynold Chambered Depollution Mixer or
Psi Tunneling Reconstruction Healer
Parametric
Solver
1G->10G
POS Engine
VPN Engine
SLR Engine
Resolution
Controller
Sigma->Lambda
The Machine
Quantum
Computer
Potting
Display
Vision
Imperial
Enclosure
The Transducer
Sigma: Std e.g. Moles
Lambda: Nominal
e.g. Rockwell

5.6. Rohs – Computer Rejuvenate Housing

Y798. Two Essential of Human Kind & Currency Ransom (Post)

SKY i.e. Climate Treasure – African due Industrial ransom – Dollar Shortage
AIR i.e. Energy Robustness – Germanic due Education ransom – Won Shortage
ALT. HEAT i.e. Economic Rotation – Asian due Food ransom – Sterling Shortage
WATER i.e. Hygiene Immunity – Jewish due Ether Time Zone ransom – Token Shortage
LIGHT i.e. Social Fellowship – Semitic due Wisdom ransom – Yuan Shortage
LAND i.e. Crime Disruption – Chinese due Legacy ransom – Pound Shortage

"Do not get any gold or silver or copper to take with you in your belts— 10 no bag for the journey or extra shirt or sandals or a staff, for the worker is worth his keep. Matthew 10:9-10
腰包里不要带金银或铜钱。在路上不要带行囊，不要带两件衣服*，也不要带鞋子和手杖，因为工人配得自己的食物。马太福音 10:9-10

Y799. Building Control System (Whitepaper)

PI&D

1. E&E Circuit Breaker System
Golden Purity Carbon Dating

2. Sewage Routing System
Horse Power per Boundary Hygiene Level

3. Water Filtered Tank System
Ionised Reynold Currency Duty

4. Antenna & Security System
Bandwidth UV conductivity rate

5. Smoke & Air conditional Humidity System
Cloud Meta Mol Psi Mach Mapping

Y800. Building Material Protocol Rohs (Whitepaper)

A. Isomer 6per: Organic Chemistry Mechanism
i. DNA #43 Meta: Adam & Eve a.k.a. Esther
ii. DNA #42 Meta: Abraham a.k.a. Zechariah
iii. RNA Blueprint: Noel a.k.a. Elza
iv. Viral Replicator: Jacob a.k.a. Habakkuk
v. Codec Skeleton Model: Joseph a.k.a. Nehemiah
vi. mDNA Percentile Meta: Malachi a.k.a. Hosea

B. Isotope 5per: Organic Carbon Dating Purity (Universal Constant Pi 64Bit Industrial Grade, PC rating)
i. Coral Quarts (3G): CPU
ii. Oyster Calcium (4G): Network
iii. Gold Germanium (5G): GPU
iv. Wax Diode (6G): Bios
v. Tungsten Nickel (7G): APU

C. Isometric 4per: Organic Chemical Thermal Microstructure
i. Graded Core (Skew 4per) – Thermal CP Rating (Progressive), e.g. Grand Piano (Hymn in Eb)
ii. Schism Core (Yaw 3per) – Moles PC rating (Harden), e.g. Hard Rock Piano (Christmas in G)
iii. Alternate Core (Offset 6per) – Meta CAP rating (Mixed), e.g. Acoustic Piano (Classical in E)
iv. Filtered Core (Shift 5per) – Parametric CPPC rating (Plain), e.g. Jazz Piano (Homemade a.k.a. Hope Music in D major)

Y803. Fraud Material Identification & Industrial Revolution the Correlation 3 times (Whitepaper)

A. 18K Gold, Silk & Silver Old Land 土地 (64bit) Soldered Board 金首饰镀金电板 (High Cryptography as in Sound & Vision Field) – For Girl, Industrial Graded, CP rating (Leviticus Food Protocol, Halal)
Hospital, Sky – Adventist
Thessalonians SG
Fixed DNS, 2G Buddhism Triband Pureland, 5G Union Maxwell Pluto Galaxy e.g. Santa Claus vs Joseph (6G, NASA Broadcast Hub MACAO)
Remastered
Industrial Revolution I – Ship Rudder Windy & Light Mill, Resin & Cultured Glass the Machine as Component Era 1850s'
Chronicle Founder: Faraday Discovery of Electricity Activity Bandwidth the Resistor Ohm Law

B. 22K Gold, Glass & Bronze Fresh Air 空气 (44bit) Wiring Cable 抵押金电缆 (High ESD Voltage as in Organic Timer)– Green Camp Graded, CAP rating (Deuteronomy Firewall Protocol, Dogma)
Mafia, Universe – Utopia
Philemon MY
Fixed IP, 3G Agnostic Triband Renaissance, 4.5G Great Eastern (Revelation) e.g. Messi vs Pilate Pontius->Messiah (9G, Populated Census Logistic Merchant SG)
Legacy
Industrial Revolution III the Final – Aircraft Celsius Boost Radiator, Quantum Feedback Control e.g. Developing Chromed Dust as well as Brushes Suction, Nylon & Fur Textile
Chronicle Founder: Silk Making was initially started since After Christ A.D. 100 years, by Fashion Culture and Chinese Tang Palace.

C. 23K Gold, Steel & Gold Sunlight 阳光 (High Conductivity as in Vision & Hearing) (11~12bit) Commuting Wire 纯金电线– For Man, Commercial Graded, PC rating (Numbers Meta Protocol, Levy)
Army, Land – Promised Land
Titus CN
Range DNS, 1G Islam Triband Paradise, 4G Pentecostal Calendar Exodus Supernova Blackjack e.g. Chris vs James->Christ, (7G, Hollywood Meta Tax Office TW)
Produced
Industrial Revolution Start – Train Alcohol Formulated Combustor, Timbered & Stainless Steel the Universal Device as Framework Era 1600s'
Chronicle Founder: Catalyst Discovery by Moore's Moles Law

D. 24K Gold, Stone & Platinum Drinked Water 水 (24bit) Diaphragm'less Plating 沙金金箔膜片 (Low Melting Point as in Vibration Resonance as

replace the Water alone – Blue Camp Graded, CPPC rating (Exodus Carbon Bill Protocol, Rohs)
Mental, Sea – Oriental
Timothy INDIA
Range IP, 2.4G Inaugural Heaven Triband Eden Garden, 10G Emmanuel Dogma South Polar Rohs e.g. Joshua vs Luther->2nd Coming Jesuit, (8G, Aegian Musician Complex MY)
Anthropology
Industrial Revolution II – Rocket Jet Compressor, Diamond Filtered & Wax Polished the Pollution Era 1950s'
Chronicle Founder: Diaphram'less Vacumn Membrane Invented by Heart Regulator Ironman

Y805. 4 Type of Housing (Forum)

A. Oriental: Fashioned Class e.g. Fence Terrace Secret Garden
i.e. Fig Tree, Operation
Pentagon
24K Tower

B. Adventist: Private Class e.g. Tunnel Mansion, Mountain Lake Garden
i.e. Swan Lake, Communication
Chapel
18K Hall

C. Promised Land: Poverty Class e.g. Landed Condominium, Moon River Eden Garden
i.e. Fruit of Life, Fellowship
Cathedral
22K Hub

D. Utopia: Public Class, e.g. Staged Harbour, Olive Tree Sky Garden
i.e. Lylith Flowers, Administration
Tabernacle
23K Host

Y813. Politic Evolution Programs (Census)

i. Dynasty (Royal Education)->(Renaissance Cultural i.e. Micro Economic Popularism), **3G International Space Stations, Bells Ionised Weather Control Network, Lambda Dragon (Titanic) vs Satan**

ii. Democracy (University Education)->(Star Exploration i.e. Talents Ransom Bank Notes), **4G Rainbow Bridge, Polarised Moon a.k.a. Twin Galaxy, Network Commuting Satellite, Sigma Unicorn (Rambo) vs Demon**

iii. Fasci Marxist (Academy Education->(Colonisation Treaty i.e. Meta Clock Calendar Reconciliation), **5G New Christmas Nativity, Hubble Telescope, Sigma Dog (Batman) vs Lion**

iv. Nationalist (Public Education)->(War & Wall i.e. Christian Treasure), **6G Meteor, Galileo Telescope, New Christian Reconciliation Nativity, Lost and Found Sheep (Spiderman) vs Dragon**

v. Nazi Marxist (Home Education)->(Industrial Revolution i.e. Gold Purity), **7G Star Dust Comet James Webbs Telescope, Utopia@Terrorism Threat, Repel Lamb (Superman) vs Fox**

vi. Republican (Private Education)->(Economic Revolution i.e. Tax Model), **8G Supernova the New Star Discovery i.e. Black Jack, BBC@Tsunami Threat bench on 18 Rohs or Green Card the Climate Protocol, Lamb (Chris)(2012') vs Man of Sins**

vii. Federation (Fashion Education)->(Music Evolution i.e. Formatted Music Notes), **9G Beidou Star Pluto Planet, Old A.D.@Genocide Threat bench on Halal or Levy the Logistic Protocol, Sheep (Messi)(Jurassic Park) vs Ancient Dragon**

viii. Monarchy Democrat (Royal Medicine)->(Computer Evolution i.e. Satellite), **10G South Polar Crabmachine Surface Satellite, A.D.@Nuclear Threat bench on Dogma or Fleas Bank Note the Firewall Protocol, Goat (Jesuit)(Star War) vs False Christ/False Prophet/Devil**

Glossary

1. The Economy & Politic (Jerusalem Foundation)

Timeline of end world: Zigzac, and anytime.
Mastermind: Racist related, not money related for sure.
Marriage Supremacy: Non Specific Marriage, preferential on Bread over Love. Advocate Testimony.
Marriage Autonomy: Specific Marriage, preferential on Love over Bread. Advocate Ministry.
Political Wing: Far left point to conservative, far right point to radical.
Superstitious: Crime Disorder, Erotic, Heresy, Multi-theism, e.g. Crime.
Idealism: Economy Disorder, Idealism, Serve two God, Trinit-ism e.g. Terrorism.
Materialism: Social Disorder, Secular, No Righteous, Monotheism, e.g. Raping.
Popularism: Civil Disorder, Nationalism, Idolism, Agnostic, e.g. Fraud.
Marxism: Marxism, Far Left wing, Socialism.
Fusionism: Fusionism, Centre Left wing, Religionism.
Nazism: Far Right wing, Materialism.
Fascism: Fascism, Centre Right wing, Racialism.
Neo Nazi: Economy Disorder as well as Anti-Chinese. Enterprise Syndicate incl. Qing Syndicate. Anti-Chinese.
Fasci Japan: Civil Disorder as well as Anti-God. Crime Syndicate incl. East India Company. Qing Regime.
Nazi Germany: Social Disorder as well as Anti-Semitic. War Syndicate. Anti-Semitic. Soong Sister Dynasty.
Communist Crime Disorder as well as Anti-Christ. Terrorism Syndicate incl. Islamic State. Qing Conspiracy Basement.
Russian Bratva: Linkup to Taliban & Mind Control Society. Custom Committee.
East India Company: Linkup to Al-Qaeda & Casino Society. Hospital Committee.
Klu Klux Klan: Linkup to ISIS & Mental Research Institute. Casino Committee.
Italy Mafia: Linkup to Islamic State & Falungong syndicate. Bank Committee.
IQ: Intelligence Quotient, Identity, Statistical.
AQ: Adversity Quotient, Thing, Parameter.
CQ: Creative Quotient, Time, Directional.
EQ: Emotional Quotient, Place, Geometrical.
Goal Oriented: Two-way thinking. Versus analysis. Duality.
Task Oriented: Alternative way thinking. Brainstorming. One direction.
Result Oriented: Multiple-way thinking. Independent analysis. Concurrent.

Process Oriented: One-way thinking. Critical analysis. Sequence.
Nationalism: Three party formation a.k.a. 3 People's Principle. Human Right inclined. e.g. Protestation.
Pan Democracy: Alliance formation, Coverage inclined. e.g. Money Campaign.
Democracy: Coalition formation, Two party political formation. Credit Inclined. e.g. Presidential Election.
Republican: One party formation. Population inclined. e.g. General Election.
Federalism: Slaved & Commercial Crime inclined. Charity model. Government Monetary.
Commonwealth: Erotic & Intelligence Crime inclined, Labour inclined. Investment model. Family Monetary.
Capitalism: Labour & Criminal Crime inclined. Supply Chain model. Individual Monetary.
Communism: Servicing & Civil Crime, Servicing inclined. Franchised model. Partial Government Monetary.
Reunification of Religion: Oppose to Renaissance. Religion Unity. Economy Recession. Shia Islam commission, e.g. Babylon.
Economics transformation: Oppose Industrial Revolution. Economy Booming. Agnostic Islam commission, e.g. Nile River.
Cultural Renaissance: Belong to Social Disorder. No racial discrimination and racial reconciliation but Anti-Semitic. Economy Downturn. Sufism Islam commission, e.g. Aegean Sea.
Industrial Revolution: Technology foundation as well as infrastructure upgrading. Economy Crisis. Sunni Islam commission, e.g. Babel Tower.

Continue on Next Page

1a. Published (Croyalflush Ministry Foundation 锄大地事工基金会)

Socialist: Think Tank->Antichrist
Non Socialist: Fund->Gentile
Democratic: Scapegoat->Biblical Villain
Politic: Psychology->Edge
Religion: Criminology->Credit

Duty Exception per Capita: Identity
Tax Legislation: Bureau
Identity per Calendar Lapsed: Misconduction Degree
Identity per Calendar: Seal Number the Ethnic
Type of Calendar: Seal Event per Religion
High Seal Number: Heavy Bureau Tax

Bureau Tax: Capita Volume the Population Census
Bureau Organisation: Promote Religion Unity the Extreme Islam
Crime Disruption Ministry: War Organisation and Crime Organisation.

Military Regime: Continent per Capita
Politician Party: Cryptography per Capita
Bi-Parliament: Career Selection
Hierarchy Parliament: Career Founder, per Capita
Nationalist: Laboratory e.g. Science Data Analysis
Democracy: Office e.g. Technology Development
Fasci Socialist: Church e.g. Ecumenical Standard Initiative, the Judification
Marxism Socialist: University e.g. Engineering Standard Initiative, the Framework

Private Mail: Intelligence + Broadcast i.e. CCC
Public Published: Meta Tither + Broadcast i.e. Real Value
Fashion Big Ante: Commuting + Meta Tither i.e. Truth Value

Continue on Next Page

2. The Ethnicity & Business (World Bank)

Jew 3 tribes: Zion i.e. Irish, Hebrew i.e. Jew, Semitic i.e. Jude.
Semitic 12 sects: Any ethnic pre-selection for salvation among each racial formed the definition of Semitic 12 sects. e.g. Israel, Hongkong, Dubai, New Delphi, total 12 sects.
Copyright: Foundation, Improvised version.
Patent: Pillar, Authentic version.
Copycat: Platform, Ugly version.
Trademark: Legacy, Beautified version.
Service Mark: Fundamental, Draft version.
Improvised: a.k.a. Jazz, Original Chord, Advertisement Music. incl. Poetry song.
Retro: a.k.a. Folk, Original Melody, Sheet Music. incl. Church song.
Indie: a.k.a. Pop, Original Tone, Album Music. incl. Christmas song.
Unplugged: a.k.a. Rock, Original Tempo, Concert Music. incl. Hymn song.
Classical: a.k.a. Symphony, Original Rhythm, Recording Music. incl. Praise song.
Dali 大理: Suspended Scale. Indian, Mainland Chinese 华夏民族, incl. 闽, 澳, 台
Dunhuang 敦煌: Harmonic Minor Scale. Chosen, Diaspora Chinese 中华民族, incl. 津, 港, 新
Shangri La 香格里拉: Diminished Scale. Korean, National Chinese 大汉民族, incl. 浙
Green Island 绿岛: Harmonic Major Scale. Japanese, Mandarin Chinese 大华民族, incl. 京, 苏, 粤
Dagger 小刀会: Augmented Scale. Thai, Oversea Chinese 华侨民族, incl. 桂, 蒙

Broadway: 1 per Bass, Portuguese incl. African, Portuguese
Quartet: 4 per Strings, Spanish incl. Jude, Greek, Spanish
Band: 3 per Choir, French incl. Germanic, Irish, French
Accompany: 2 per Piano, Dutch incl. Celt, Dutch
Orchestra: 5 per Drum, Italian incl. Jew, Italian
Boiled; Baked: Pork & Seafood, South America, Macao,Nanjing.
Steamed; Stew: Mutton & Venison, Europe, Taiwan,Tianjing.
Stir Fry; Roasted: Poultry & Vegetable, Australia, Malaysia,Shanghai.
Fried; Grill: Fish & Egg, United Kingdom, Hongkong,Beijing.
Braised; Gravy: Beef & Duck, United States, Singapore,Shenzhen
Chinese Medicine: Therapy e.g. Acupuncture.
Drug: Herbs e.g. Supplementary.
Vaccine: Cures e.g. Immune.
Pharmacy: Tonics e.g. Nutriology.
Quarantine Management: Testing e.g. Laboratory.
Regenerative Medicine: Chinese Medicine, New Age Medicine, Psychiatry Drug, Herbs, Therapy Oriented.
Nutriology Medicine: Western Medicine, Surgical Medicine, Pharmacy Supplement, Tonics, Anatomy Oriented.

Hexagram Code Numeric, Cipher, Superimposed, Chronicle to Name Etymology.
Morse Code Alphabet, String, Thread, Festival to Name Etymology.
Light Code Symbol, Echo, Histogram, Capital to Name Etymology.

Continue on Next Page

2a. Published (Chinese Reunion Fellowship 新中华府)

Blueprint: Practise, Theory, Model, (Data Mark, Kelvin Mark, Hall Mark).
Chronography: No Clan, Diaspora
Calligraphy: Non Orthodox, Schism
Nativity: No Shoe, Critic
Carrier: Best Treasure Ethnic
Pilot: Best Intellectual Ethnic
Treasure Integrity: Human Right Act
Intellectual Integrity: Intelligence Act

Food Scheme: Class A1: Tamed, Class F4: Seafood, Class C: Herb, Low<High Class: Mouse<Bird
Energy Scheme: Class A1: Hormone Bill, Class F4: Carbon Bill, Class C: Poison Bill, Low<High Class: Calories<Calcium Bill
Pentecost Legacy Scheme: Class A1: Wage Duty Carrier, Class F4: Compensation Duty Carrier, Class C: Salary Duty Carrier, Low<High Class: Devotion<Burden Duty Carrier, i.e. Cryptography
Meta Genetic Scheme: Class A1: Culture Renaissance, Class F4: Humanity Renaissance, Class C: Heritage Renaissance, Low<High Class: Industrial<Technology Renaissance, i.e. Nativity
Quantum Treasure Scheme: Class A1: Advent, Class F4: Oriental, Class C: Promised Land, Low<High Class: Utopia, i.e. Chronography
Esther: Star Dust Stream, Time tax
Ezra: Star Dust Pressure, Heat tax
Nehemiah: Star Dust Wind, Quantum tax
Economic Conspiracy: Christian Persecution. Third World. Junk Technology, a.k.a. Renaissance Era.
Heritage Terrorism: Anti Semitic. First World. Junk Culture, a.k.a. Contemporary Era.
Royalty: Depend on Geology, Space Footage, the Merchant Age. The Intelligence.
Loyalty: Depend on Geography, Spiritual Channel, the Marketing Standard. The Broadcast.
Lent: Depend on Demography, Time Zone, the Insurance Ranking. The Calculating.

Natalie: Clock Wise Meta, Class A1, 88 Graded Weighted Piano
Intellect: Anti Clock Wise Meta, Class C, Flute
Sheep: Anti Clock Wise Meta, Class B, Guitar
Goat: Clock Wise Meta, Class C, Violin
Lamb: Clock Wise Meta, Class B, Cello
Gentile: Clock Wise Meta, Class F4, Keyboard Piano

Lent Legislation Law: Lent, Loyalty, Royalty
Intelligence Fee: The Value counted from Tax of Duty whenever equilibrium.
Intelligence: Carrier Meta
Land Property Value: Footage Milestone per Boundary Datum

3. The Religion & Theology (Vatican Organisation)

Theorem: Business Management, Telecommunication, Pseudo Science; Commission.
Theory: a.k.a. Law, Astronomy, Arts, Applied Physics, Nature Science; Ethic.
Theology: a.k.a. Canon, Politics, Risk Management, Operation Management, Social Science; Spirit.
Doctrine: a.k.a. Principle, Medicine, Music, Logistic, Architecture Science; Ethnic.
Dogma: a.k.a. Theory, Martial Arts, War Strategic, Criminology, Psychology; Erotic.
Principle: Genealogy and Medicine. a.k.a. Bible Character. i.e. Ethnic.
Law: Archaeology and Astronomy. a.k.a. Bible Story i.e. Ethic.
Catechism: Constitutions and Politics. a.k.a. Canon of Bible.
Justice: Criminal Law and Anti-Social Law, against Crime Disorder i.e. Criminal Justification.
Justification: Holy Confession, Forgiveness, Faith, Speak in tongue.
Sanctification: Holy Baptism, Repentance, Love, Pentecost.
Glorification: Holy Communion, Offering, Hope, Theosis.
Regeneration: Holy Sacrament, Righteousness, Work, Christian Perfection.
Testimony: Its harms than benefit, do ministry than testimonial for Orthodox Christianity nor for Atheism.
Orthodox Christianity: Apostolic Church where Ministry of God as well as Missionary is valued. Teaching of Overview and strengthening of Christianity Fundamental.
Lutheran: Churches that value Salvation by Faith alone as well as value 'No racial discrimination', it is disrupting social harmony if too vigorous. Teaching of Basic and strengthening Christianity Foundation.
Christianity Reforming: Separating Lutheran Church out of four division of Christianity denomination.
Trinity: One to Three, Three entity regulated to Core.
Monotheism: Three in One, Three core regulated to one entity.
Erotic Defect: Man or women whoever compromise sex before and/or after marriage.
Adultery: Man or women pursuit love for money or pursuit love for sex before and/or after marriage.
Evil Spirit: Whoever contributing to social disorder as well as strong will of destruction conscious holistically.
Anti-Semitic: Link to Nazi Germany, in which any illegal activities contributed to disrupting Jew as well as those Pre-selection Jew from each racial group, for reconciliation.
Religion Unity: Link to Christianity Reforming, The endeavour of Orthodox Christianity to form alliance with Islam as well as other Orthodox religion.
Heaven: Link to Social Disorder, the place called itself heaven is the place where no social disorder and forward to progressive high civilisation and to perpetual life.
Christian Science: Conclude in Scientific theology as well as Creationism belief, a.k.a. Fundamentalist.

Pseudo Science: Conclude in Telecommunication as well as Revelation belief, a.k.a. Pentecostal.
Salvation: Those who are Completed Christian as well as those who equip with Christianity equivalent methodology. There are no single way but many way lead to salvation.
Canon: The rule in and rule out of targeted number of books from Old Testament as well as from New Testament to form an interconnected logical loops in other to fulfil the teachings of Salvation of Christ.
Climate Disaster Readiness: Conspiracy of Tsunami, targeting to block the evangelism of Christianity as well as targeting disrupt human civilisation by minimising the global emergency readiness in all activities to disperse human connection e.g. Social Disorder, Anti-Semitic, Religion disharmony, Terrorism, Erotic defect, World War.
Nuclear Weapon: High destructive, low occurrence nuclear weapon, literally it has no threatening advantage over other mass destructive weapon. But it can be illegally misused out of control the crude oil economy as well as preventive measure of escalating to World war.
Social Disorder: Link to Nazi Germany, in which a society harmony is disrupted in terms of social connection as well as social affiliation on weighing to leader of society.
Social Security: Liability on privacy/freedom that cause threat, depends on social sensitivity, popularism & social ranking mismatched i.e. social disorder.
Semitic Persecution: Social Disorder Activity, incl. Quarantine, Job sanction. Same to Christian Persecution.

Continue on Next Page

3a. Published (Christian Organisation 基督徒集团)

Goat: Intellect, Word Prison, Semitic
Sheep: Tither, Trojan Horse, Christian
Lamb: Natalie, Colony, Anointed

Scapegoat: Terrorism Ransom to Semitic, Memory Defect, Alternate Semitic
Antichrist: Chronic Failure Ransom to Christian, Erotic Defect, Extra Christian
Gentile: Disaster Ransom to Stakeholder, Poison Defect, Grading Reincarnated

101 Righteous Sheppard Dogs: Duty Ransom, Sigma, Lion
99 Lost and Found Sheeps: Threatening Lawsuit, Omega, Horse
500 Repel Lambs: Guinea Trial, Lambda, Dragon

Cult a.k.a. Oriental Democracy: Buddhism Noel, Christian Persecution, Democracy Academy, Alternate Camps
Communist a.k.a. Fasci Socialist: Utopia Series, Stakeholder Persecution, Royalism Military, Extra Censors
Islam Prayer a.k.a. Aqueda: Islam Noel, Semitic Persecution, Constitutional Congress, Grading Streams

Hierarchy Traitor: African, Nazi Fasci
Regime Repel: Jew, Mafia
Cells Schism: Manchu, Syndicate

Footage Binding: Capita Suit, Chronography
Cryptography Milestone: Capita Scheme, Calligraphy
Footprint Clock: Capita Clan, Demography

Redemption: Body Lapsed
Atonement: Spiritual Mileage
Judification: Fellowship Margin

Holistic Science: Biblical Conjugation
Pseudo Science: Mechanics Reaction
Systematic Science: Mechanics Mechanism

Montage Intellectual: Universal Spectrum Histogram
Social Montage: Political Evolutional Scheme
Social Hierarchy: Moses code Iteration number

Rabbi: Academy Scholarship, Queen the Inaugural
Puppet: Congress Stakeholder, King the Final
Idol: Market Moderator, Jack the Least

Meta Clock the Diaspora, Byte: Reactors Programs, the Clustered Stereotype,

Isomer, Timber Product Graded, i.e. Heat Flux
Timer Clock the Heat, Era: Mechanism Series, the Stereotype Bind Number,
Isotope, Metal Element Trajectory, i.e. Heat Carrier
Sets of Clock the Voltage, Value: Mechanics Generations, the Genealogy Wave,
Isometric, Silicon Energy Releasing, i.e. Lumen Value.

Chronicle: Eschatology Calendar Atonement Byte per Gross Capita a.k.a. Ether Stellar i.e. Solar Stellar, the National Treasure, Hygienic the Tax Agency. UN, WWF, KMT, World Bank. Publisher Certification Protocol
Jobs: Ecumenical Judification Era per Gross Capita a.k.a. Solar Wave, the Universal Energy, Administration the Space Agency. NASA, WHO, NATO, Vatican. Medicine Scheme Cover
Exodus: Industrial Framework Redemption Value per Capita a.k.a. Ether Dust i.e. Solar Dust, the International Economy, Intelligence the Bureau Agency. CIA, FBI, ZION, Jerusalem. Wage Deficit Package

Adventist or Eschatology Calendar: Covenant, Universal Sins Protocol e.g. Etymology
Judification or Ecumenical Catechism: Doctrine, Constitutional Sets of Law, e.g. Ecumenical
Economic Treasure or Etymology Semitic Congress: Dogma, Orthogonal, Aerial, Pentecostal, Holoscopic, e.g. Holysee

Democracy: University
Royalism: Academy

Ritual: Quantum Carrier Metric. The Conversation Bill for Real Value.
Legitimated: Judification Platform. e.g. Platform Saving Account. Distrust Account Platform. Allergy Account Platform. i.e. The Famous Ecumenical of Vatican contrast with the HolySee.

Stellar Head: Community Leader and Spiritual Leader.
18 Luohan: The Fasci Community Leader of 18per. e.g. Pope, Bishop, Islam Prophet or Islam Spiritual for Jihad, the Revenge.

Continue on Next Page

Continued

Federal per Capita: Spiritual Cast Out the Derivative Products due Misdoing and Perceiving-ness the Aggregate. Timely Kick out High Bonding Product. (The Commuting Generations)
Gross Capital per Clan: Marriage or Max Tither, Food Compound Profit Sharing Ranking (The Inaugural Sky High Nativity)
Nativity Mileage per Capita: Carrier Tither, Commuting Energy Cost (Land Wall)
Nativity Milestone per Gross Capital: Timezone any One to One Couple only, Homogenous, the Time Lock Metric (Eden Garden the Schematic to Next and Original, i.e. One Lord, Two Lord, Trinity Lord, and Multiple Lord, no more Lord)

Security Bank, Federal Bank: Option Security Branch and Trading Security Branch
Investment Bank, World Bank: Property Bonds Investment Branch and Labour Investment Branch

Sea, Harbour:
Dust, Axis Carrier Tither:
Meta Tither:

World of Renaissance to Oriental: Ban Civilisation of Humanity (i.e. Sky Community) in Marriage to Tither Marriage, Islam Ally
World of Herald to Adventist: Promote Civilisation of Culture (i.e. Land Community) in Tither Carrier to Fallacy to Distortion Carrier, Buddhism Ally

Sodomy: Pilgrim
Virginia: Anabaptism

Continue on Next Page

4. The Technology & Science (United Nations Agency)

Upstream technology: Fundamental/Innovative technology rely on academic.
Downstream technology: Foundation/Frontier technology rely on experiment.
Health Law: i.e. Systematic Biology a.k.a. Robot Technology, Hardware. 12 symbol, 12 Robot Organs as well as 12 Human Organs corresponding to 12 Chemistry Compound, incl. 3 Energy Mechanism.
Psychology Law: i.e. Systematic Psychology. a.k.a. Robot Technology, Software. Intelligence, Emotional, Creative and Adversity Quotient. incl. Scalar Computer, e.g. Measuring software, Quantum Computer, e.g. Solver software.
Pharmacy: Enzymes, Hormones, Mucosa, Insulin corresponding to Stem cell, Vitamin, Analgesic, Steroid.
Artificial Intelligence: Technology about Automation and Robot. If Civilisation reach peak, beyond that would bring humanity destruction, point to Medicine Science and Telecommunication Science.
Augmented Reality: Technology about Machine and Robotic. If Civilisation reach a stalled situation, above that would bring humanity advanced, point to Logistic Science and Combustion Science.
Virtual Reality: Technology about Simulation and Computer. If Civilisation reach crisis, below that would bring humanity downturn, point to Engineering and Computer Science.
Economy Load: Quantity of Mainstream Population, as High quantity of Mainstream population comes
along reduced Economy Bill.
Mainstream population: The Bandwidth of telecommunication is the measure of Mainstream population.
Life expectancy: The measure of telecommunication bandwidth of a person, point to their endervour, ministry and life expectancy.
Harvest Gain Theory: i.e. Calendar Theory, a.k.a. Relativity Theory. The relationship of (Bandwidth of telecommunication)^power of X/(Half-life) proportional to (Harvest Gain). Analogy from Farmers and Fisherman. Half-life is a constant, but it depend on the gravitational field, i.e. moon phase. These contributed to Operation Management e.g. Agriculture, Food.
Chaos Theory: i.e. Time progression Theory, a.k.a. Entropy Theory, 2 way time progression, Closed form system, Predictable, Entropy, series events, Automatic Guiding, End loops, Analogy from Combustion Science. These contributed to Transportation e.g. Satellite, Jet.
Reality Decryption Theory: i.e. Augmented Reality Theory a.k.a. Feedback Control Theory, Algorithm Engine (Sensor, Encryptor) transfer to Combustion Engine (Actuator, Synthesizer) then to Film Engine (Gauge, Decryptor), Analogy from Computer Science. These contributed to Augmented Reality e.g. Mining, Construction, Nuclear Reactor etc.

Light Code Theory: i.e. Time Phase Theory a.k.a. Engineering Drafting Theory, 4 Distance Formula of 9 Planet, yield Hexagram Code to Moses Code then to Light Code. i.e. Metric system to Imperial system then to International Unit. These contributed to Engineering e.g. Telecommunication, Manufacturing.
Inheritance Decryption: There are Long generation, Wide generation interpolated to Orphanage generation, Broken generation and Ancient generation, which stick to inherited of father or mother gene. This constitute to the fundamental of medicine, called contagious disease.
Rocky Effect Decryption: There is a guarantee that mainstream will always remain constant, if there is guarantee victory; it has to uphold anything what confirmed and assured into equation of fighting. This constitute to the fundamental of manufacturing, called quality management.
Heaven Decryption: No more than 45 network. 3 network is coherent host. Each network has own translator as well as reflection. 18 same of a kind parallel network, 24 isolated series network. This constitute to the fundamental of social science, called mass media.

Continue on Next Page

4a. Published (Croyals Medicine Agency 石医医学署)

Quantum Treasure: The Three Biblical Treasure from Initial Christian Judification to Final Revelation Judgement, which is grace alone, many alternative way.
Economic Treasure: As above.
Christian Mathematics: Technology
War Insight: Weapon Methodology to Quantum Treasure
Criminology: Biblical Sins
Ending of Biblical Villain: Biblical Sinner Penalty
Hybrid Engineering: Military Technology

Christian Politics: Social Science
Social Engineering: Social Scamming
Christian Medicine: Genealogy Technology
Christian Finance: Economic Methodology to Quantum Treasure
Classification of Ethnic: Ethnic Labelling & Graded
Politics Evolution: Series to Economic Harvest Reinvention

Biblical Application: Doctrinal Training
Christian Education: Theology
Puritan Music: Church Music

Third World: The Utopia, defined by Stone Heritage Oriented. As this involved Trojan Horse, Word Prison, and Colony, correspond to Erotic Defect, Taste Defect, and Pollution Defect. Upside down of this is Oriental.
First World: The Renaissance, defined by Paper Heritage Oriented. As this involved Technology Frauding, Technology Hacking, Technology Scamming. Upside down of this is Promised Land.
Folks Revolution: The Cow Boy suit. White Supremacy. Pilgrim Heritage, Catholic Schism.
First of May Revolution: The Labour suit. Holistic Science, Fundamentalist Schism.
Thither Revolution: The Angel suit. Meta Correlation Schism, Puritan Schism.
Seal & Pirate: The Blueprint Decryption of Ancestry Heritage inheritor, Anointed Religion Duty.
Flagship & Imperial: The Blueprint Projection from Professional Technology Prestige, Specific Religion Prestige etc.
Signature & Testimonial: The Blueprint Cast out of Election Semitic Heritage and Ecumenical Church Anointed.
Official & Credential: Nativity & Meta. Possession of Authentic Inherit Blueprint. This begin with Migration/Exile of Major Prophet to Exile/Migration of Minor Prophet. i.e. Primary Atonement, Corner stone, and Redemption.
Meta Law: Directional, from top to down.

Dead Sequence: One major Schism and one minor schism and one diminished schism.

Continued

Utopia Beta: Industrial Revolution to Third World Manual Mode Engineering the Metrology Administration Products Fulfilment, a.k.a. Home Office Revolution. The Major Schism the 1st Dead Route. i.e. Democrats.
Promised Land: Industrial Revolution the 3rd, to Utopia Final Autopilot Mode Engineering the Robotic, a.k.a. Natalie Career Revolution i.e. Semitic Career. The Minor Schism the 2nd Dead Route. i.e. Nationalist.
Renaissance: Industrial Revolution the Final Pilot Mode Engineering the Simulation, to First World, a.k.a. Intellect Career Revolution i.e. Christian Career. The Diminished Schism the Fire Lake Route. i.e. Republican.
Oriental: Ecumenical Maturity Milestone yield the Industrial Revolution the Original, to Automatic Holistic Engineering Mode e.g. Infrastructure Cast Out. The Major Schism to Resurrection the 1st. i.e. Democracy.
Advent: Eschatology Events. Industrial Revolution the Greatest Time Lapsed, to Man Made Reinvented Engineering Mode e.g. Telecommunicational Medicine Projects. The Minor Schism to Resurrection the 2nd. i.e. Monarchy.

Footprint: Cast Out, Holoscopic the Axis of 3per
Foot-ink: Plotted, Aerial the Axis of 2per
Footage: Projection, Pentecostal the Axis of 1per

Sky App: Remote i.e. Client, Official & Legitimated Signature
Land Rover: Hostage i.e. Protocol, Certified & Tested Flagship
Sea Gate: Hosting i.e. Port, Opened & Operating Seal

Remaster: Cast Out, Orthogonal the Axis of 6per
Jeopardy: Plotted, Homogenous the Axis of 5per
Pilgrim: Projection, Holistic the Axis of 4per

Profit Ruler Grading: 7th, 6R, Marketplace, Commercialised
Margin Ruler Grading: 1st, 4R, Summit, Legitimated
Datum Ruler Grading: 6th, 3R, Dispatch, Publicised
Progressive Grading: Generic, 1R to 3R, Cluster, Cultivated

Latin Numbering: Generations
Roman Numbering: Series
Greek Numbering: Dimensional

Firefox: Landing
Netscape: Mapping
Explorer: Rolling
Errata 17Jan2023

Stellar: Universe Crystallisation, Organic Lambda #1-14

Sterilisation: Energy Crystallisation, Chemistry Continued

Stellalisation: Social Crystallisation, Chemical

Artefact Boomerang: Quantum and Graded Schism merging is Lock 1 years, the 500 iteration.
Decorate Boomerang: Alternate to Extra Schism merging is Lock 10 years, the 5000 iteration.

Reynold: moles number X Constant= Meta Tither per Pi Number
Meta Scaled Boundary Footage, Property Value = Based on Reynold Number

Snow Train: Partial the Event Occurrence Rate
Transformer: Trinity the Intelligence Knowledge Value
Iron Man: Mono the Environment Hue Depth
Crabmachine: Multiple the Spiritual Nerve Power

Laboratory Estate: Headquarter the 11th
Tower Landscape: Less 1 Pillar

Errata 16/17/18/25/27Apr2020, 19/21/23May2020, 8/14/16/21/22/23/27/28Jun2020, 3/9/11/24/30Jul2020, 13Aug2020, 15Sep2020, 13Oct2020, 25/27/28Oct2020, 9/13/16Jan2021, 13Mar2021, 12Oct2022, 30Nov2022, 4Dec2022, 2Jan2023, 11Jan2023, 23Jan2023, 7Feb2023, 12Feb2023

Chinese Royal Flush™ Oriental Tonguepost 锄大地东方当铺

Caution: Some scam disguised Cult as Online Church. Prohibited worshiping Online Church, even with Covid-19 Epidemic, don't follow the trend, please take Spiritual carefully. No one can worship God without Tabernacle and without Fellowship.

"..You shall not take the name of the LORD your God in vain..." Exodus 20:1-17

Disclaimer: We are a Profit Organisation, rooted in Adelaide, Melbourne, Klang, Singapore, and Established in Johor Bahru. We very much like a Christian School as well as a Christian Solution Consultancy. We had accumulated certain extent of experiences & knowledge-base from Practical in Engineering, Politic, Music, Criminology, Theology, Economic, and Christian Education incl. Christian Mathematics, Christian Arts, Christian Science, Christian Music and Christian Law. We are serving upstream God Ministry and selectively downstream public ministry, e.g. Product Invention, Politic Revolution Campaign, Music Show, Crime Disruption Project, Theology Publication etc. You may find us in High Level teaching as close as Christian School by Christian Education Heritage. You may find us in High Level problem resolve as good as Christian Solution Consultancy in solving the real world Economic Science Development Issue. We are highly efficient, with nearly zero funding, we managed struggle to success, but with your devoted or little donation would shape us in many ways to sustain or speedy heading to victory against wicked power and evil network.

What we belief is Holistic the Hue Made of King. And this is in-regardless of Pollution
but purely Imagination of Schism of Hue. And for anyone has this Schism in Gross has
the Hue, and this is Freedom and Freedom. The Dream a little Dream and become Real
Value in the Cloud one day. Called Adventist i.e. "I Want This".

Precaution of Misconduction of Manual Adjustment or Judgemental e.g. Lawmaker for
Legislation, not about Opportunity but Risk Escalating, and this make Hue into Rainbow
6. Instead of that, promote of Humanity Weapon Treaty is the Biblical Way for Differ the
Salvation i.e. Permittable Max 10% Tither. Anything greater than this and momentum
consider Holysee of Highest Majesty.

Imprint of any Spiritual is Extra Mistake and more Mistake, and Yield no boosted Beneficial.

The Telecommunication Fouls, in Humanity Crime and War Crime, in Production of
Biscuit and Carbon Bill for Blocked Vulnerable Channel for Hygience Allergy as Prime.
*Chinese Literacy please translate from English which is the Whole Book Pillar.

Errata 28Jan2023

你的后裔和女人的后裔也彼此为仇，女人的后裔要伤你的头，你要伤他的脚跟 创世纪 3:15
Serpent Meta is Clock Wise. Eve Meta is Sarah the Egyptian Queen the Pharisee.

- About Croyalflush Ministry Foundation, 关于活石事工基金会

A. Our Vision:

Preserved Scientific Theology. i.e. Building the **Religion Unity Pillar**.

B. Our Mission:

Economic Science Research to Exit Federalism the Ecosystem Economic. i.e. **Salvation to whole Chinese Ultimately**.

C. Our Job:

Promote Long Hierarchy Company & Revealed as well as Opposed all kind of Christian Persecutions. i.e. **Advent of God Kingdom Decryption**.

D. Our Ministry:

Guideline to Disruption Climate Change Conspiracy. i.e. **Advanced Civilisation Threshold**.

E. Our Organisation & Milestone:

E1. Christian Education Aggregate
Published 'Fundamental of Christianity' website for Evangelism to Non believer and Reformation for Reborn Christian by Christian Science.

E2. Theology Aggregate
Published 'Matthew Gospel Commentary', 'New Theology Application' , 'Six Bible Myth', 'Nine Portion of Theology' Articles.

E3. Criminology Aggregate
Published 'End World Backup Plan' Book content incl. Crime Syndicate Network Revealed & Christian Persecution Revealed & Crime Conspirator Disruption Guide.

E4. Economic Aggregate
Published 'Light Encyclopedia™, Book total 700 Pages, content incl. Culture Heritage, Religion, Applied Physics, Social Science to Economic Science.

E5. Music Aggregate
Published CroyalPiano™ Music Encyclopedia, variety of Arrangement and Composed Music & Song. incl. Chinese Classic, Korean Pop, Piano Theme, Hymn Retro.

E6. Politic Aggregate
Published 'Editorial Articles' of each Country issue as well as Global Issue, to reach Ministry Agenda.

E7. Engineering Aggregate
Published CroyalDesign™ Machine Gallery incl. Cleared Leading Design & Manufacture Milestone for making Travel Gadget Grade Mobile Phone, Kitchen Appliance Grade P.O.S. Computer and Business Instrument Grade Meter.

F. Join Us

We are just small scale Educator & Consultancy Organisation, to survive we ought to grow up to moderate organisation for gaining power and influences. There are many phase and way you can join. If you saw this notice and feel interested please don't hesitate contact the Croyalflush Ministry Foundation's Secretary for delivering your interest, and there are alot of new jobs can be assigned.

Those Organization or Individuals who had partnership or contributes, this is the remembrance. We much care for any mis-leading or fallibility of Religion Belief, if yes, please let us know before you make report and take necessary action against us. Thank you!

The harvest is plentiful but the workers are few. Matthew 9:37
收割的工作多，而工人少。马太福音 9:37

About Founders 关于创办人

There is nothing but guide, please use at your own risk. The one who failure in life is the one who followed. Trust your heart.
这是专业的参考手册，滥用后果自负。人生失败者往往都是跟随者。要忠于自己的感觉。

- About Founders 关于创办人

Personal Miles Stone

On the dark side called myself God Father or Underground Theologian, has multiple Criminal Minority, incl. stealth, fraud, fighting, hardcore, gambling and hacking. Deliverance from acute surgery, fatal car accident, stage dismissal, job dismissal, tinnitus, temporary disable, marriage mistake, marriage failure to social blacklisting, a life regret to my ex-girlfriend, in which constituted the reason of writing **Foundation – of End World Backup Plan**, for Crime Syndicate Key Person Disruption.

Aspired in Mechanical Engineering, successfully graduated in Australia Top Tier University regretful defer 1½ year, Coupe with over 12 years Design Engineering skills in R&D Firm Since 2003′ Portfolio with over 12 type of **Pillar – CroyalDesign of Machine Gallery**, retired at Forty years old amid apologetic to my Parents. Looking to startup Micro Retail Business as Making a Living for 2nd Part of Career Journey.

Thanks to Wikipedia.com, then founded "**Platform – Light Encyclopedia**" from 2013′-Present, a Light weighted but Comprehensive Encyclopedia (total 700 pages). Hence of the Manual Book, founded Non-profit organization Croyalflush Ministry Foundation Since 2011′, progressively building Spiritually Diplomacy Ministry against Villain of Christianity, Rival of Christianity & Cult of Christianity.

On top of that, since childhood has cultured music skills, and then accumulated vast amount of on stage performing experiences in Chinese Orchestra, Folk Music Cafe, and Church Worship Ministry. Impromptu recording include over 21 type of Music Genre published as "**Legacy – CroyalPiano™ Music Encyclopedia**".

Credit to Reformed Church and Fundamentalist Church, was trained as an Apostolic writer for Advanced Theology, Biblical Application to Global Ministry, Author of "**Croyalflush – Fundamental of Christianity**" for Christianity evangelism and reformation website since 2017′.

The Founders included My Parents, Father and Mother, in which involved in Legacy in terms of Inspiration on many topics in this books.

个人里程碑

在黑暗面自称为教父或地下神学家，有多个小型犯罪记录，包括偷窃，欺诈，打架，嫖妓，赌博和骇客。从急性手术、致命车祸、舞台解雇、职场解雇、耳鸣、暂时残废、婚姻错误、婚姻失败到社会黑名单被释放，对前女友来说是一生的遗憾，因此构成了撰写《世界末日备份计划-基础》的原因，即犯罪集团关键人物捣破。

渴望修读机械工程，并成功毕业于澳大利亚顶级大学，遗憾推迟一年半毕业，自 2003 年以来拥有超过十二年在研发公司的设计工程技能，累计荣获超过十二种设计产品奖项里程碑。收录在《石医设计机器画廊-梁柱》，四十岁退休的我对父母道歉。展望于我的微商零售生意当作后半生的职场生涯。

感谢 WIKIPEDIA.COM，从 2013 年至今创立了《活石光百科全书-平台》，轻量但全方位综合百科全书（共七百页）。因这本秘笈书，成立了活石事工基金会始于二零一一年，渐进的与基督教的反派，基督教的对手，基督教的邪派，建立属灵外交事工。

除此之外，从小学习音乐，并在华乐团、民间音乐咖啡馆和教会崇拜事工积累了大量的舞台演出经验。即兴录音包括超过二十一种类型的音乐曲风，《石医钢琴音乐百科-遗产》。

归功于归正派教会和原教旨主义派教会的培训成为使徒作家，专长于高级神学与全球事工圣经的应用等，自 2017 年，创立了基督教福音派和归正网站，《活石基督教-概论》。

创办人包括我的父母，爸爸和妈妈，参与献出思想启发遗产包括其中在书本出现的多个标题。

Made in the USA
Columbia, SC
19 May 2024

34857598R00085